Escape from Codependent Christianity

by: **Dr. James B. Richards**

Impact Ministries
Publications Department
3300 N. Broad Place SW
Huntsville, AL 35805
(205)536-9402

*Not affiliated with Impact Publishers, Inc.
San Luis Obispo, California*

Impact Ministries
Publications Department
3300 N. Broad Place SW
Huntsville, AL 35805
(205)536-9402
Fax: (205)536-4530
E-Mail: Impact4God@aol.com

Cover photo by:
Jonathan T. Hall, Huntsville, Alabama

ISBN: 0-924748-10-9
First Printing, September 1996
Second Printing, June 1997

Other Books by Dr. Richards:

Taking the Limits Off God
The Gospel of Peace
The Prayer Organizer
Supernatural Evangelism
Grace: The Power to Change
Leadership That Builds People, Vol. 1
My Church, My Family:
    How to Have a Healthy Relationship
    with the Church
Satan Unmasked

Information also available about:

Impact International School of Ministry
    Resident Program
    Correspondence Program
    External Degree Program
Tape & Book Catalog (free)

*To receive any of the above,
call or write today:*

Impact Ministries
3300 N. Broad Place SW
Huntsville, AL 35805
(205)536-9402 ● Fax: (205)536-4530
E-mail: Impact4God@aol.com

Impact International School of Ministry

Impact International School of Ministry has been training leaders since 1983. We are training a new breed of leaders to reach the world like never before.

The greatest complaint against the church today, is that it is not relevant. Most of society does not believe the church recognizes or understands how to meet the needs of modern man. Studies indicate that most recorded church growth in America is actually people who are simply changing churches. The church is failing to make a real *impact* on society with the gospel.

At Impact International School of Ministry, we are training leaders who understand and know how to minister to the needs of our society. Truth remains absolute, but the application of truth must be modified to be appealing and relevant to those we wish to reach. Jesus never presented the Gospel the same way twice. He was always sensitive to the needs of those to whom He ministered.

At Impact International School of Ministry we believe the church should "hold fast" to the truth, while being flexible enough to be effective in society. We help you prepare to reach your world and minister to their needs. Our department of relevant ministries is always forging ahead to understand and develop ministry techniques that work.

Call today for a personal consultation. Let us help you develop a strategy to fulfill your call to the ministry.

Call or write today for information:

**Impact International
School of Ministry**
3300 N. Broad Place SW
Huntsville, AL 35805
(205)536-9402 ● (205)536-9876
Fax: (205)536-4530
E-Mail: Impact4God@aol.com

Table of Contents

(continued on next page)

Section 4: The Cure

SECTION 1:
CODEPENDENCE
IN RELATIONSHIPS

SECTION 1:
INTRODUCTION

Codependency tends to affect man at his area of deepest need, meaningful relationships. We give into these tendencies thinking they will get us the secure, loving relationships that we desire only to find that we destroy them by the very methods we employ. By employing the strategies of codependency, we not only hurt the ones we love, we draw out the very worst in their behavior. Often, our codependent tendencies plunge everyone around us into those tendencies as the only way to survive emotionally.

Codependency touches every human being alive. We will all, at one time or another, exhibit some codependent tendencies. Being aware of those tendencies and avoiding them will help us in our relations with others. Coming to understand the motivation behind those tendencies will help us to conquer the problem.

Section 1 identifies many codependent tendencies and helps us understand how they are affecting our relationships. More importantly, in this section we get a firm grasp on the root cause of codependency. For the first time, we are given the tools to conquer the problem.

A codependent lifestyle is a miserable, fearful life. From never feeling secure, to the need to always be in control, the extremes of codependency fuel the chaos and pain in our lives. As you read each chapter, take the time to prayerfully consider where it identifies you and make the appropriate decisions to put an end to this cycle in your life.

1

CODEPENDENCY: WHAT IS IT?

It seems that as every year goes by, new diseases of the mind and body emerge. Medical science is working day and night trying to develop cures for new viruses that threaten the very existence of humanity. Likewise, those who deal with emotional pain and conflict continually seek new answers to the problems that plague the emotional lives of the human race.

There seems to be a million different kinds of emotional problems out there. Some sectors of society try to deny their existence, but the effects of emotional dysfunction abound whether we admit it or not. There are experts in the medical, social and religious fields who try to explain away problems as if they were willfully conjured up by society for some selfish reason, but such denials reflect a lack of realism, concern and understanding. In fact, such attitudes reflect a part of the problem.

There are others who recognize the myriad of emotional conflicts and they are seeking a million different answers for the million types of problems that exist. This attempt to find answers is quite overwhelming for the patient and practitioner. It puts the ability to solve the problems out of the reach of the one in need. It causes him to place his hope in the expert who sometimes becomes an extension of the problem.

While there are thousands, if not millions of different emotional disorders, there are only a few answers. A healthy emotional life functions around some very simple realities. Coming to understand and accept those principles will cause a person to find the freedom that has so long eluded him. Regardless of a person's particular beliefs, society itself bears witness that there are certain immutable truths that will cause one to experience peace of mind, a sense of well being, and healthy relationships with others.

When these truths are violated, everyone suffers. The individual suffers and all of his relationships suffer. People around him are affected and society as a whole suffers. The violence, domestic instability, drugs, and many of the physical sicknesses that exist are the product of man abandoning these principles.

The medical profession is very quick to admit that a large percentage of the physical illnesses they deal with are stress related. Stress is a non-measurable phenomenon that is created from a non-physical source. In other words, it is the product of the emotional life of the individual. It is created from thoughts, beliefs and opinions. It is negative emotional energy that ultimately affects the physical body.

Stress in the body can turn into a destructive energy causing high blood pressure, migraines, cancer, and immuno-suppressant diseases of all types. In the emotions, stress can be turned into anger, hatred, worry, or fear. These emotions can turn into violence and other acts of aggression that destroy relationships between husbands and wives, parents and children, friends and neighbors. It is time that the human race begins to observe the truth that has been proven for thousands of years. We must abandon our own foolish thinking and look beyond ourselves for the help that we need. We must manage our life and emotions in a different way if we expect to see different results. If we are in emotional pain, we cannot continue to think and believe the way we always have and expect our situation to change. Psychiatric drugs will numb the pain, but not solve the problem. Learning to cope will cause us to shut our eyes while the problem grows. Trying to change others will only create more problems. We must face the only sure source of peace and relief. We must deal with ourselves.

In the 80's a terminology began to emerge describing what seemed to be a new emotional problem: codependency. This terminology was first used to describe people who were dependent upon someone who was dependent upon some destructive substance like alcohol or drugs. Even though the codependent was not a substance abuser, they were dependent upon someone who was. Therefore, they were co-dependent. It was as if they joined in and participated in that addiction through a relationship with the person who was addicted.

Over the years, the concept of codependency developed. Now it takes several pages to describe the tendencies of what is labeled as codependency.

A simple definition of codependency would be: to depend on someone for something that we have no right to expect from them. The codependent often looks for other people's approval for a sense of self-worth. They may depend on others to make their decisions. They may look to others for happiness. But whatever they are looking for, the key is that they look to others for something that other people cannot truly give them.

Melody Beattie does a great job of identifying codependent tendencies in her book, "*Codependent No More.*" The only problem is, you will certainly find some codependent tendency that you often resort to. Few people in our society are free from some codependent influence. Codependency is actually encouraged and nurtured in certain aspects of our society.

Codependency is not a new thing. Only the name is new. This is a 90's terminology for an age old problem. Actually, it is one of the oldest problems in the Bible. It is at the root of every inter-relational conflict. It is the underlying and often unseen force that works behind every addiction. It is the cause of aggressive behavior. It leads one person into total aggression and another into total passivity. It is deceitful, it changes form so as not to be easily detected. In some circles it is rewarded because it can disguise itself as commitment, dedication and loyalty. It can appear as love, but is only discovered as its toxicity destroys a marriage. It can make a man faithful to one woman, even though he hates her. It can make another man unfaithful to his wife, even though he loves her.

Codependency can work its way into every good thing and destroy it. It can become the leaven that leavens the entire loaf. It can become the strange quirk that causes a good business to fail. It can be the unpredictable phenomenon that destroys every relationship. It can be the unseen "demon" that seems to follow you around to destroy every good thing that happens in your life. It is the root of why you lose control in certain settings. Whether you are a classic codependent or not, you will find that it is when you give into the codependent tendencies that destruction and pain come into your life.

2

OBSERVING CODEPENDENCY

For years, I have observed codependent tendencies in the lives of the people who came to me for counsel. It took many years before I was able to catalog the similarity of actions. It took even longer to come up with a compassionate understanding of the problem.

For years I noticed that the majority of people, including myself, repeated the same destructive patterns over and over. Whatever problems a person had before they surrendered their life to the Lord were basically the same types of problems that they had forever. Often these problems would not be acted out the same way but they would be motivated by the same tendencies.

I noticed that women who dated abusive men would reach such a place of pain that they would break up with the current abuser, only to date another person with the same problem. In the end, they would usually marry a person who was abusive. The odd thing, however, was that the person they married may never show one tendency toward violence until they were married. Then the mask would come off and the unsuspecting woman would be trapped.

I often wondered how a person could end up with so many abusive men. How could people repeat the same mistakes over and over again? It's like the young man who has been in a little trouble at school. It's not too serious yet. He doesn't really want to be a bad kid, but he is magnetically drawn to other young boys who will lead him astray.

It's like the man who's sitting across the desk from me. He is heartbroken. He is crying and sobbing, "Are all women sluts? Why is it that every woman I love is unfaithful? This is the same thing that happened in my last marriage. I will never trust a woman again!" I'm sitting there wondering, "How do you find such bad wives?"

Or it's like the person who gets married only to find that their mate is a closet alcoholic. Or the woman who finds this is the third man in a row who has been a sexual deviant. Or the man finds that this woman, just like the last three, is a clinging vine. Or the woman finds that her husband is just like her controlling, dominating father. Or a struggling alcoholic walks into a room of three hundred people and the person he ends up talking to is also a struggling alcoholic.

What is happening? Did God decide He would torment me by continually putting these people in my path? Is there an invisible demonic force that is planning my life? Is there a sign on my back that says, "I have a weakness for abusive women"? Why do I keep ending up in the same situation over and over again?

Unfortunately, our experiences forge our perceptions and our perceptions guide our decision making. If our perceptions were formed from incorrect evaluations of data, all of our decisions will be bad. Because of the way we interpret all of this, we create a perception (belief system) that ensures we will stay in the cycle of pain.

I have actually known men who decided that

all women were bad. I have known women who reach the conclusion that all men will hurt you. I've known people who decide that love will always hurt. I've seen too many people decide that God must be bad and mean. I've seen people decide that they must have done something terribly wrong for life to be treating them this way. I've seen people decide that they would never be happy and actually believe they should not be happy.

All of these are wrong conclusions derived from incorrect perceptions based on a wrong interpretation of the facts. There is one common denominator in all of these beliefs: "The problem is outside of me. I am not responsible. I have no control over these events. This is someone else's fault." Yet, the one and only constant factor in every person's problem is themselves. I have been present in every one of my problems. Like the country song says, "Where ever you go, there you are." No matter where I go or what I do, I am always there.

I am the constant factor in all my problems. If I move to a different city, get a different job and a new set of friends, and the same thing happens there that happened before it is time that I view it differently. I must admit that I am somehow involved in this. I must do what is nearly impossible for the codependent to do. I must recognize that the problem is in me. But I should do it in a healthy, constructive way.

As I dealt with these tendencies in people, I came to realize that we all have certain beliefs and opinions; we have certain needs and we display certain characteristics that always attract the same kind of people to us. It has become second nature for us to pick up on the way people walk and talk.

We have become able, on a subconscious level, to read the verbal and nonverbal behavior of people. And, we are drawn to a particular behavior without realizing why.

In my own life, I realized that I was always in relationships with women whom I despised. I would always end up with the "clinging vine." I could not understand how that happened. If there was anything that repulsed me, it was a clinging, smothering person. Yet at some point in every relationship, the blinders would come off and I would realize that I was snuggled up to a clinging vine who had her tentacles wrapped all around me.

No matter how angry I felt toward that person, I had to admit that I was the one who had gotten into this. But why didn't I see it at the beginning? Were all these women so deceptive or was I so blind? Looking back, I realized that these were not mean, vicious, deceptive women. There was something that attracted this kind of person to me. There was also something that was attracting me to this kind of person. What was it?

As painful as it was, I realized that these women appealed to my ego. When I first met them, they thought I was everything (that should have revealed something to me). I liked that. These women thought I could do anything. I liked that. Everything about the relationship appealed to my ego.

After I blindly rushed in, it was not long before they wanted me to make decisions for them. At first that was all right, it revealed how smart I was. Then they wanted to see me everyday and that was all right, too, after all I was such a desirable person. This sick progression moved right to the stage of "I need you." Then it usually took the quantum leap to "I'll kill myself if you leave me."

In reality, I didn't believe I was smart. I didn't think I was attractive and I didn't think I was a good catch. But when someone else expressed those things to me, it met a need in my life. I actually began to depend on that person to meet a need that should be met somewhere else. I was as codependent as they were, I just wasn't as helpless. My problem was just as real and *I* was the constant factor in every romantic scenario that turned out that way.

Our needs blind us to reality. Every con artist in the world knows this. If he has what you need and if he can get you acting in greed, you will close your eyes to all rationality. You will ignore the warning signs along the way. You will walk openly into the snare. He won't even have to deceive you. Our need and our greed to have someone else meet that need blinds us to reality.

In every counseling session with a person who had been in a codependent situation, they were able to look back and say, "All the warning signs were there. I should have seen them." However, our need and greed blind us. Greed is that factor of selfishness that is so concerned with getting our need met that we enter into what I call willful confusion.

In James 3:16 it says, *"For where envying and strife is, there is confusion and every evil work."* The word *envy* is from the Greek word *zeal*. Zeal is when a person is ambitious. The NIV[1] translates it as *selfish ambition*. When there is selfish ambition, there will be confusion. I can't see things as they are as long as I am moving in greed.

My needs do not have to move me to greed.

There is nothing wrong with having a need. The problem emerges, however, when I depend on someone else to meet that need for me. I can never look outside myself to discover what should be found in my own heart. The codependent has developed a pattern of looking to others to meet the needs that can only be met in his own heart. Because certain needs cannot be met by others, the codependent is blinded through desperation. He begins the cycle of pain.

1 *New International Version of The Holy Bible,* Zondervan Bible Publishers, Grand Rapids Michigan

3

FINDING MY SOURCE

Codependency has grown in the world because the world has rejected the source of life. Likewise, codependency has grown in the church because the church doesn't trust the source of Life. Colossians 2:10 makes one of the most profound and unbelievable claims of the entire Bible: *"And ye are complete in Him, which is the head of all principality and power."*

We attest to our lack of believing and experiencing this verse every time we depend on someone to meet a need for us that can only be met "in Him." The world only understands the root of codependency to a degree. Because they do not consider God as a viable factor, they can never find the real solutions. In fact, God being left out of the psychological equation was the cause of codependency to start with. Leaving Him out of the healing equation is like putting a band aid on a cancer.

Without God, people can experience a degree of relief, but they can never experience real fullness of joy. An alcoholic, for example, can get clean, but he cannot get free without God. He will simply fill the void with meetings, therapy or some other substitute. That substitute enables him to stay off of alcohol, but the rest of his life he must remind himself that he is merely an alcoholic in recovery.

Please understand, I am in no way condemning a program that gets people clean. I have great respect and admiration for those who develop and participate in programs that get people clean. They have often done more for the needs of society than the church has. They are bringing a degree of relief and peace to the individual who has lived his life trapped in an addiction.

Some of the most codependent people I have ever seen, however, are people who are in recovery. They become dependent on the recovery process and never really get free. They have simply transferred their dependency from something totally unacceptable to something that is a little more socially acceptable. But the truth remains: this is not freedom, it is only relief.

It is more than annoying when the codependent in recovery is able to so quickly identify and point out the codependent tendencies in others. As if that was not enough, he insists that everyone should participate in his group or receive his type of therapy because, after all, it is doing him so much good.

It is not the intention of codependent support programs to nurture this kind of attitude. This is merely the extension of the codependent's problem into his current environment. We cannot blame the program for the weaknesses of the people. After all, Christians do the same thing. Christians try to shove God down the throat of the world in a very offensive way. Yet our own lifestyle is the proof that the world does not want our God. God has had this problem with His people for thousands of years. *"For the name of God is blasphemed among the Gentiles through you, as it is written."* Romans 2:24.

The problem is not necessarily the system, it is the people in the system. The Old Testament law had all the information a person would ever need to maintain good friendships, have good marriages, raise perfect children, succeed at business and have an all around good life. But it had a weakness. . . THE PEOPLE! *"For what the law could not do, in that it was weak through the flesh. . ."* Romans 8:3.

Even the law, which was perfect in content, had a weakness: the people! It would be more than arrogant for us to think that we could devise a system that was better than God's. It would be more than presumptuous to assume that our system could perfect people when God's system could not perfect people. The law itself never perfected anyone. *"For the law having a shadow of good things to come, and not the very image of the things, can never with those sacrifices which they offered year by year continually make the comers thereunto perfect."* Hebrews 10:1.

The sinner, who continually attended all the right meetings and said and did all the right things, was still a sinner. So, no matter what his accomplishments, he stood before God and man and continually reminded himself, "I'm a recovering sinner." I may be a sinner who is doing better; I may be a sinner who doesn't sin like I used to; I may be a sinner in a way that you cannot see with your eyes; but in my heart, I am still a sinner.

Likewise, the alcoholic, drug addict, sex addict or codependent will always be just that, until he is set free. He may be in recovery. He may have been clean for ten years. He may be living a clean life, but he is still an alcoholic, drug addict or codependent at heart. And it is essential that he remind himself that he is just that. The day that he forgets that he is an alcoholic, sex addict or codependent will be the day he allows himself to run risks that he cannot handle. It will be the day he falls.

Don't condemn the person who can only stay clean by remembering. Even the Christian who is clean, but not free, had better remind himself of his problem or he will fall. Being a Christian and experiencing the power of God in a specific area of life are entirely two different things. The Christian knows in his heart whether he is merely clean or if he is indeed free.

He will not be free until he experiences the power of *"In Him ye are complete."* The theology of that verse will make one knowledgeable, but knowledge puffs up. *"The Kingdom of God is not in word but in power."* 1 Corinthians 4:20. Until we have experienced the power of truth, it is just information. That information may motivate us to get clean, but only the power can make us free.

Christians are just as bad as any other group about becoming codependent on our methods and on our leaders. We look to people and methods because we do not really trust God to bring us wholeness. We may trust those who represent Him, but we do not trust Him. We trust in our doctrines and creeds as a substitute for trusting in the character and faithfulness of God.

In reality, codependency is when we depend on anyone to do for us what only God, Himself, can do. People around us can contribute to our freedom, but they cannot be the source of our freedom. A method or a system can contribute to freedom, but it cannot be the power that brings freedom. Freedom comes when something happens in my heart with God because I have truly made Him my source. I must experience the liberating power of God or I am not free. I am simply clean. But I cannot experience that power unless I trust God. He must be my source. He must be my all in all. I must find my completeness in Him, not the method, not the messenger. . .in Him!

The Chinese have a saying, "If you think you can learn from a book, don't buy the book. If you think you can learn from a teacher, don't get a teacher." Books, teachers, and programs are not the way. Jesus is the way. Our books, teachers, and programs should point us to the way, if they do not point us to God as our source, they become part of the problem.

4

KNOWING GOD

"Because he hath set his love upon me, therefore will I deliver him: I will set him on high, because he hath known my name." Psalms 91:14. There is one basic reason that people do not love God; they do not know Him. There is one basic reason people do not trust God: they do not know Him. There is one reason people do not look to God as their source: they do not know Him. There is one reason the world is in a mess: THEY DO NOT KNOW GOD!

Understand, I am not saying that millions of people have not *met* Him. Jesus said,*"Take my yoke upon you and learn of me."* Matthew 11:29. Salvation is the *beginning* of a relationship, not the climax. At salvation, we have the opportunity to become involved with God in a very personal way. This is the beginning of knowing God. At the end of his life, the apostle Paul still made knowing God the primary goal of his life. His ministry was not first, knowing God was first.

Only through knowing God can we experience Him as our source of liberating power. Paul said, *"I want to know Him and the power of His resurrection."* Philippians 3:10. If the message does not point me to a personal relationship with God, it will point me away from God. If the method does not move me toward personal involvement with

God, it will move me away from God. All of the churches, preachers, prayers and programs should encourage me in the pursuit of a personal relationship with God. They should never become a substitute.

Jesus said, *"And this is life eternal, that they might know thee the only true God, and Jesus Christ, whom thou hast sent.* John 17:3. To know Him personally is the source of life. Not mere life as we know it, but the quality of life that He has.

I am not saying that people do not know certain aspects of God. But as a whole, we have rejected the picture of God that Jesus brought to the world and instead we have opted for a religious, legalistic concept of God. Jesus showed us God in a way that we could understand and relate to. Hebrews 1:3 in the NIV says He was *"the exact representation of God."*

If the theology that I "twist" out of the scriptures does not confirm what Jesus showed me, I am wrong. If what I believe about God makes Him hard to trust or hard to love, I am confused. This is not the picture that Jesus came to portray. Most of the messages preached Sunday after Sunday are totally incompatible with the portrait that Jesus presented of God. The result of all of this departure from truth is that people have a hard time trusting and depending on God. We are nurturing the very problem that Jesus came to solve.

God created man in His likeness and image. We are social, emotional, relationship-oriented beings. There is something inherent in our psychological make up that causes us to look outside of ourselves for certain needs. For example, we need love from another being. We determine our self-worth by the value others place on us. The desire for validation outside of ourselves was God-given. It is present in every human being.

I believe God factored this in so we would look to Him to meet those needs. He is the only one who will ever love us unconditionally with a perfect love. It is the realization of His great love and value for us that should give us our sense of self worth. All of this should work to bring us into a healthy, willful relationship with God. He should be the source of meeting all of our deepest needs.

Because God is love, because He never changes, we have the opportunity to experience constant, positive input. But if we do not trust Him, if we do not know that He is loving and merciful, if we do not recognize the value He has for us as demonstrated at the cross, we will look somewhere else to have our deep needs met.

There is no one who can love us perfectly or constantly but God. Because the love that others have for us fluctuates, our sense of worth and confidence fluctuates. We are up and down with the inconsistencies of those we depend on. Our inconsistencies then become justified by the inconsistencies of others. I am no longer responsible for what happens in my life. I do not have an anger problem; the problem is that other people do things to make me angry. I do not have a depression problem; other people do things that cause me to be depressed.

This codependent scenario is even more complicated by our attempts to earn the love and acceptance of others. This is a great source of bitterness and anger. As a social, emotional, relationship-oriented being who has certain needs that can only be met from an outside source, I decide to look to you to meet those needs.   You may have even committed to meet those needs. But I soon realize that if I don't act right, you are not able to make me feel loved. You can't show me love when I offend you. So I work hard to do all the right things. But, since you are human, you have bad days occasionally.   So you don't meet my needs. Now I not only fail to feel loved, I have done what I think should have earned me something and you won't give it to me. You are now the justifiable focus of my frustration and anger. You are the one who is causing me my pain.

The codependent is always looking to an imperfect sc arce to give perfect love. He is always depending on people for something that only God can do. As people fail us, we become more afraid to trust.   By the time we are presented with the concept of God, our hearts have been so hurt by trusting others that we are afraid to trust God. Our painful experiences, coupled with all the preaching about an angry God, make Him the last being in the universe that we would look to for love and acceptance.

God has made peace with man through the Lord Jesus (Colossians 1:20) and He has taken the law that was against us and nailed it to the cross (Colossians 2:14). By the finished work of Jesus, we now stand before God holy, blameless, and unreprovable (Colossians 1:22). He demonstrated His great love for us in the fact that Jesus paid the full price for our sin (1 John 4:9-10). He has freely given us His love so that we would have no fear of Him at all (1 John 4:18). All of this makes it possible for us to come boldly before the throne of grace (Hebrews 4:16).

There is no reason that we should not trust

God and draw near to Him. He has made the way open. Because we do not know *Him*, and we only know our unscriptural opinions, we are afraid to trust Him. We have judged God to be untrustworthy. We have believed a lie about God.

The law said, *"Thou shalt not make unto thee any graven image, or any likeness of any thing that is in heaven above, or that is in the earth beneath, or that is in the water under the earth."* Exodus 20:4. The reason we should not make any graven image is because He is our God, there should be none before Him.

In the Old Testament, people would cut down a tree and fashion it into what they thought the image of God was like. Then they would bow down to the image and say, "You are my god." Our problem is not that we cut down a tree and fashion an idol, instead we tend to cut down the image of God that Jesus presented and replace it with a concept that has been imposed upon us by religion. Then we say, "This is what God is like. I can't trust Him."

We are like the man in the parable with one talent. His opinion created the obstacle. He assumed his master to be hard and mean. Those false images made it impossible for the servant to trust his master. Likewise, we create unscriptural opinions about God that make it impossible to trust Him. We don't know Him,we only know the image of Him that we have created.

God is the great I Am. He is all we need. He is omnipotent and omniscient. He is for me and not against me. He is the source of my life. He is the spring from which flows all the rivers of life. He is my source of joy, peace, confidence and self-worth. Others can participate in these feelings, they can contribute to them, but no one else is the source of those feelings. They can affect these feelings, but they cannot take them away. One way of identifying the source of any emotion is to determine who can take it away.

God reveals Himself to us by His name. As I read and pondered the names of God, I realized that all of His names were good. He didn't have any bad name. He did not have a name that reflected anger or rejection. All of His names reflected peace, love, healing, victory, and dozens of other life-giving attributes.

Ultimately, God revealed Himself through Jesus. Too many times, I have incorporated some doctrinal position that portrayed a concept of God foreign to what Jesus represented. I found a God I could trust and draw near to when I made Jesus the interpreting factor of my beliefs. When I looked at the way He treated people, I accepted the reality of what He said in John 14:9 and I found a God I could trust and draw near to. *"He that hath seen me hath seen the Father. . ."*

When I realized others can contribute, but God is my source, I found a freedom from depending on people that changed every relationship I would ever have. I couldn't be controlled and I had no need to control. I appreciated people's approval, but I didn't need their approval. I felt good when people expressed love for me, but I was not depressed when they didn't. I had a new constant in my life: the love and acceptance of the unchanging God.

5

CONTROL IS THE GOAL

Control is a major issue for the codependent individual. After all, if you are the source of my happiness, I must control you. If I don't control you, you may do something that will cost me my happiness, security or self-worth. I can't run the risk of that kind of pain.

The codependent can never have a truly meaningful relationship with anyone. Every relationship is entered with the expectation of what the other person can do to meet my needs. Every person (victim) becomes a possible source for meeting these essential needs in my life.

This mentality produces a deep self-centered relationship. Others are only of value to the degree they can meet my needs. This is why the codependent finds himself in bad relationships over and over again. He is so consumed with the possibility of getting his own needs met that he never notices many of the important warning signs.

Because the codependent sees something that they think will meet their need, they fantasize what the relationship will be. They don't see the person, they see the imaginary person. They see how this person can meet their need. They never really get to know the person, nor does the person ever get to know them. They have a fantasy in their mind that they must make come to pass.

Numerous times, I have counseled with people who were contemplating marriage. When they would describe their potential mate to me I would be thinking, "Are we talking about the same guy, because I've never seen that side of him." As they would continue to describe their relationship, I would realize they were describing their fantasy.

The codependent has a fantasy of marriage. When they find someone, they simply paint that person's face on the picture in the fantasy. All too soon, they find that it is not the person they love, it is the fantasy. When that person turns out to be different from the fantasy, they either quickly move on or they try to take control and create their fantasy. Seldom do they actually build a relationship.

While we all have standards of what we want and expect in marriage, there should be some room for variation. When we meet someone, we should become friends, develop a relationship and see how it will unfold. See if we like what it becomes. See what it will become without our control. Only then can we actually know the other person.

Because the codependent has a fantasy, they don't know for sure if their fantasy will make them happy. They never experience different things with different people. They simply try to force everyone into the fulfillment of their fantasy, thereby cheating themselves out of opportunities to grow.

As long as we control a person, we can never know them. We only know the image we have created. Usually we don't do that well on our creations, we never seem to get it right. We must continually recreate them. The dominant person has a need. He must be able to respect his partner. When the dominant person can't respect you, he has little value for you. After he molds you into the person he wants you to be, he doesn't respect you. After all, if you were any kind of person, you would not allow someone to control you.

The passive person gives in to your every need. This is a form of control. After a time of giving in and creating a self-centered monster, the passive person feels used and angry. They have no life of their own. They despise the aggressive control. Typical for the codependent, they never say "I gave control of my life to another." They always say, "He took control of my life."

This is a good time to point out that every behavior pattern has a slightly different way of controlling. When we talk about controllers, every subtle controller looks at the strong personality and says, "He's the controller, not me." But everyone has a way in which they attempt to control, some are just more obvious than others.

When the dominant person controls it is obvious and open. They seldom try to hide it. They openly try to control people by sheer force of character.[1] Because of this, they are usually the ones blamed for controlling while the other controllers continue in the shadows undetected. In some ways, the dominant person is the easiest to control and certainly the easiest to blame. He can't deny being a controller, he just has ways of justifying it. "I do it for your own good. I do it because I love you. I do it because you won't."

The analytical, critical thinker controls by creating standards that make him appear to be right. In his own mind, he is right. He is the "quality control" person. Since he never tries to control openly or by force of character it is easy for him to deny being a controller. He would be appalled at being accused of controlling. He's only doing what is right. It is very easy for him to shift blame. He can easily provoke the other behavioral types into extreme reactions which make them appear to be the only ones out of control. This person is diplomatic and subtle, but calculating and cold as ice when it comes to getting things done the "right" way.

Then there is the sincere, steady person. This person is loyal and personable. They have many wonderful traits, but when they decide to control they will dig their heels in and become unmovable. This person can easily function in toxic love that expects a specific response for their efforts. Failure to respond properly can produce extreme anger. Their loyalty shifts and they become loyal to accomplish their goals and not yours. This person feels very justified in involving others in the conflict for power. After all, they feel victimized. They have sacrificed so much for you and you have given so little in return.

Last of all, there is the inspirational, people-oriented, "I want you to like me" person. This is a very friendly, outgoing individual who wants to be liked. This person will go ten extra miles to make you like them, which becomes the whole problem. Regardless of the situation, in their mind it is always about them. Much of their agreeing, kindness and verbal influence is all for the response that you will give.

All of these people can be wonderful individuals and have admirable traits. I am not saying that they always do these things. This is simply the motivation and the method they employ when they attempt to control. People who are looking to other people to meet needs that only God can meet cannot resist the temptation to control. It is the only way they know to get some of their deep rooted, God-given needs met.

This entire scenario is the antithesis of true love. Biblical love is self-sacrificial. Biblical love does not lose value for self, it is just not self-motivated. Biblical love is rooted in a strong sense of self-worth. Because the individual has a deep realization of being loved, they are able to give for a motive other than response. They can actually look to the other person's need. They do not need for the other person to respond in a certain manner. They are not working a secret agenda.

Rather than entering every relationship with needs that must be met, the whole person can allow each relationship to exist on its own merit. It can become whatever it becomes. For this person, every friendship is an adventure. Every friendship is different. Unlike the codependent, the whole person does not require that every friend fit into a self-satisfying role designed to meet his personal needs. Neither does he continue to destroy relationships through his need to control them.

Every person who controls has a good motive. They can even make the motive seem noble, but know this: *control is when we invade a person's life in a way that God Himself will not do.* We must allow people the freedom to succeed and fail on their own. We can advise them in areas they ask for advice. We can ask them if they want our input, but we can never control.

Personal growth is an impossibility for the person being controlled and the person who is controlling. If I am having difficulty relating to you, I can either control you or I can grow. I can turn to God and get the grace to accept you. I develop new personal skills. I can learn more about you as a person. I can do a thousand positive, constructive things, or I can do one negative, destructive thing . . . I can control you.

Hebrews 5:14 talks about *"those who by reason of use have their senses exercised to discern good and evil."* These people came to discern good and evil by exercising their own senses. Exercise is the use of something in a way that strengthens it. We use muscles over and over to make them stronger. As we use them with light weights, we become able to handle heavier weights. Likewise, as we use our own senses, we grow in our capacity to deal with more difficult situations.

Only a fool rejects input and advice. And only a fool tries to give advice to someone who does not want it. But each person must grow by exercising their own senses. Each person must try and fail on their own or they will never grow.

No matter how noble it seems, when we control, we do it for us, not for them. Instead of asking why they won't listen to us, maybe we need to ask why we feel the need to control.

[1]   *DISC Behavioral Profile*; Carlson Learning Company, Minneapolis, MN.

6

GOD OF MY WORLD

The first act of codependency came in the Garden of Eden. It establishes the pattern for all temptation. It clearly shows codependency as one of the most basic elements of temptation. Adam's temptation, like ours, did not start with the devil, it started with his desires. No desire is evil within itself. Desires only become evil in an unbelieving heart. *"Unto the pure all things are pure: but unto them that are defiled and unbelieving is nothing pure; but even their mind and conscience is defiled.* Titus 1:15.

Desire in an unbelieving heart always leads a person away from God. The unbelieving heart does not trust God to fulfill his desires, but the believing heart takes his desires before the Lord. He looks for the Biblical way to gratify those desires. The believing heart depends on God. The unbelieving heart is always destroyed by his desires. *"The desire of the slothful killeth him. . .He coveteth greedily all the day long."* Proverbs 21:25-26.

Every desire a man has comes from a God-given need. Although it may be twisted and perverted, all desires come from something that could be fulfilled in a Biblical manner. However, when we do not trust God, when we do not believe there is a Biblical way we can fulfill those desires, then we depend on another source. This leads to sin. *"But every man is tempted, when he is drawn away of his own lust, and enticed. Then when lust hath conceived, it bringeth forth sin: and sin, when it is finished, bringeth forth death."* James 1:14-15.

God gave Adam dominion over planet earth; he ruled as a god in this world. Adam's desire to rule planet earth came from a God-given need. However, Adam had to look to God to determine what was good and evil. Adam had authority in planet earth, but he was dependent on God for the wisdom to use that authority properly. Satan came along and offered him the opportunity to rule apart from trusting and depending on the Father. *"Ye shall be as gods knowing good and evil."* Genesis 3:5. Because Adam didn't trust and depend on God, he depended on Satan (by default). Thus, we have the fall of man. As we look closer at this scenario, we may find some hints of what was working behind the scenes.

For Adam to rule with God, he had to trust God. To trust Him, he must maintain a relationship. If he took Satan's offer, there would be no need for a relationship and there would be no need to trust. At the heart of this temptation, we find man pursuing a life apart from a trusting relationship with God. At the heart of every human difficulty, we find this same unbelief. We find people who do not trust God.

The reasons for not trusting God may vary, but the end result is the same. Some people think they have to get enough faith to get God to do good things for them. They do not believe what Christ has (past tense) accomplished at the cross. Others may not believe God intervenes in the affairs of men. Still others believe that God does good things for some men, but they do not believe they are qualified just by being in Jesus. (Colossians 1:12) Regardless of the reason, unbelief is unbelief and it always leads one to depend on someone or something other than God.

After the fall of man, the first emotion to arise in man was fear. He was afraid of God. Adam expected pain and judgment from God. The result was that Adam hid from God. Unbelief led to fear, fear led to hiding from God, and hiding from God led us to depend on sources other than God to meet our deepest needs. *"There is no fear in love; but perfect love casteth out fear: because fear hath torment. He that feareth is not made perfect in love."* 1 John 4:18.

Fear and unbelief are so intertwined they are hard to separate. One produces the other. It doesn't matter which comes first, they always come in pairs. God has called us to a relationship of love. He has made a way for all of our needs to be met in Christ. We should not lack anything at all. We should be whole spirit, soul and body. *"According as his divine power hath given unto us all things that pertain unto life and godliness, through the knowledge of him that hath called us to glory and virtue."* 2 Peter 1:3. Fear and unbelief make that an impossibility.

With all that God has freely given to us, how could we walk about in such desperate need. Simple! We don't trust God. But there is a reason we don't trust Him; we are afraid of Him. There is a reason we are afraid; we don't believe He loves us with a perfect love. One cannot be made perfect in love and still have fear. The scales are always perfectly balanced by love and fear. To the degree you're not established in His perfect love, you will have fear. It is as if there is a void that will be filled with one or the other. To the degree that one is filled with the love of God, fear is driven out.

The real faith walk of the believer has nearly nothing to do with trying to get stuff from God. Think of it, this epitomizes unbelief: "Since I have fear in my heart, I don't believe that God has freely given me everything I need in Christ. I am like Adam, I somehow think He is keeping the best back from me. So I'm going to get enough "faith" to get God to give me something that He says I already have." Let's face it, if I had faith I would believe what I already have in Christ. We, like Adam, are always trying to get something God has already given us.

Faith that works by love is a faith that trusts the love that God has for us and that He demonstrated toward us in Jesus. Real faith is a response to what God has done in Jesus, it is not what we do to get God to respond to us. Real faith and confidence in every area of life comes because it is rooted in the love of God. Real believing doesn't look to how strong our faith is, as much as it looks at how strong and perfect God's love is.

Among the many things a fearful person cannot do, he cannot trust the one it fears. Those who have not established their hearts in the love of God cannot trust God. The codependent never operates from love and trust, he always works from control, "Yes, I want to be god of my world. I want control of my world." If I am in control, it sets me free from one thing I cannot do, trust. If I can control my environment I don't have to trust God. If I can control my relationships, I don't have to trust God with those relationships.

If I am god of my world, I have the right to form everyone and everything into what I desire.

Everything exists to serve me. I will not trust God to work in your life, after all, He may not make you into what I want you to be. He might make you into what He wants you to be. That may require change on my part and I am not going to change because I am at the center of my world. Everything revolves around me and my desires.

The codependent, whether an aggressive controller or a passive controller, is paralyzed, rigid and inflexible. Change is very threatening to the codependent. It is easier to try to change the world around me than it is to face the possibility that I must change. I have found my comfort zone. I must convince everyone that this is normal and they all must change.

The aggressive codependent doesn't look fearful. He may look like the most confident individual you've ever seen. He looks like he's got it all together. But he desperately fears things getting out of his control. It has been said that two of the greatest signs of maturity are flexibility and adaptability.[1] A truly confident and emotionally mature person is flexible and adaptable, he is not threatened by the changes that occur around him. The mature individual yields to others and adapts to what the environment calls for. Thus he is at peace and is able to function in any situation.

The codependent controller is neither flexible, nor adaptable. He must be in control. Everything must conform to his control so he will not be threatened. Even the passive controller who appears to be a victim is maintaining control. He is simply doing it in the way he feels comfortable. Our lack of self-control is best demonstrated in our inability to be flexible and adaptable. Our lack of self-control becomes aggression when we allow it to thrust us into controlling others. But that does make us the god of our world.

If I entrust you to God and allow you to become who God would have you to be, I will be faced with a tremendous challenge. I will have to adapt and adjust. I will have to love you, find value for you, and trust you the way you are instead of the way I want you to be. If I do not allow you to be who you are in Christ, I will never be faced with the real challenges of life. I will not have to grow if I can keep you from growing. I will not need the grace (ability) of God working in my life if you never grow beyond my ability to control.

If my world or any part of it changes, I will be forced to do the one thing I do not want to do, trust God. I will be forced to trust God for the strength to love and accept others. I will be forced to find joy and contentment in the Lord. I will no longer be able to use others for my own purposes. I will be forced to give up control.

[1] *People Smart,* Toney Alessandra, Ph.D and Michael J. O'Connor, Ph.D., Keynote Publishing Co. La Jolla, California

7

Toxic Love

Love is the deepest need a human being has and volumes have been written on the topic. But it is through the *agape* love of God that one determines a healthy sense of self-worth. It is through love that we grow. Love is the basis for our faith. (Galatians 5:6) Walking in love will fulfill every desire that God has for you. (Galatians 5:14) Loving God and loving people is the fulfillment of all of God's Word. (Matthew 22:36-40) Yet it is one of the most perverted and misunderstood subjects in the earth.

We must remember, since Adam's fall, man has determined good and evil for himself. Since we are the god of our own world, we claimed the right to define good and evil. In so doing, we have defined what love is. We have rejected God's concept of love and developed our own. It is our definition of love, however, that is causing much of the pain in our life.

Love is the deepest need a human being has. Every person is always in pursuit of being loved. It is the quality of love that is placed on us that gives us our sense of self-worth. We can't deny the need, but we have so redefined love that when we find our definition of love, it usually destroys us. We can't give it up, however, because it is such a deep need.

It's almost like a starving man finding a poisonous berry that has a sweet taste. He refuses

to believe that it is poison. After all, when he eats
it, it tastes good. Later, however, it makes him
extremely ill. Our hunger, our love of the taste,
keeps compelling us to eat it again. So we convince
ourselves that it is a good plant for food. We eat,
enjoy the taste and become very sick. We swear we
will never eat it again, but when hunger returns,
we give in to the need.

Likewise, we have a deep need to love and be
loved. We approach it from an unbiblical
perspective and get hurt. But our need for love
keeps driving us back. Since we only know love the
way we have defined it, we do the same thing over
and over, only to be hurt over and over.

Toxic love is a poisonous kind of "love." It
violates God's definition of love. It was developed
by the movie industry or by the humanists, but it
doesn't matter who invented it, it is not based on
the love of God. Only the love of God can give the
positive results that we expect from a love
relationship. Anything else will bring pain and
destruction; it is poison. It may seem to
momentarily meet the need, but in the end, it
hurts.

One form of toxic love is giving to get. The
person giving this kind of toxic love is not doing it
for the other person. He is doing it for himself. All
he wants is a desired response. His "love" is
nothing more than manipulation. It is a way to get
what he wants. He may pour on all the charm,
kindness, and gifts one could imagine, but it is a
deadly trap.

The motive for a person's action is often
revealed when you do not respond in the way they
desire. You soon discover their real motives. They
become angry. They remind you of all they have

done for you. They point out how good they are to you, implying that you should do what they want you to do. They are now using guilt as a way to get the response they desire. If this works, they may stop doing any good things to get the desired response and just use guilt. Because all they want is the response, it doesn't matter how they get it.

The person who gives toxic love is a "user" who will never be satisfied. Even when you respond in the way they desire, it doesn't satisfy the hunger in his soul. A manipulated response does not satisfy the heart like the unconditional love of God. We actually need someone to love us in a way that only God can. The user knows that you are just responding to his manipulation. Therefore, he is never really confident in your love for him. After all, if he stopped doing things for you, would you still "love" him?

This can cause the user of toxic love to swing from one extreme to the other. His resentment that you are not meeting his need for true love will overwhelm him at times. Even if your love is true, he can never really trust it. Because in his mind, your love is being bought by his actions, it is not unusual that the toxic love user places more and more demands on you to prove your love. Often, his sexual demands will become quite extreme. He expects an unrealistic loyalty. Your entire life becomes an attempt to prove to him that you love him.

Any time you fail to meet his needs, he pours the guilt on. He uses statements like, "Can't you just support me. . .After all I've done for you, you're going to leave me. . . I need for you to show me you love me." There are hundreds of guilt-producing, self-centered statements that the user of toxic love will make. If those tactics fail, he may even resort to aggression or violence. His intention from the very beginning is just to get you to respond a certain way.

The toxic love user, like any person with an addiction, is never satisfied. He always needs more to meet his need. Yet, his need is never met because he is trying to get a need met through another person that only God can meet. Even if it was possible for a person to meet his need, his methods would prevent him from ever trusting your response. "Does she love me, or does she just love what I do for her?" is the haunting question for the toxic love user. The toxic lover can never be satisfied. He may eventually need someone else on the side to convince him that he is worthy of being loved.

Another indicator of toxic love is that someone is always having their personal will violated. Sometimes the toxic love user demands sexual participation that is not satisfying or even humiliating from the other person. But it is part of the way you must prove your love. "If you love me you will. . . " is the famous line of the toxic love user.

Remember the codependent person can be an aggressive or passive controller. You may be the one forcing your desires on another person. Or you may be the one who feels you must violate yourself to prove your love. You may feel a duty or obligation to violate your dignity. "After all," you think, "it is my duty."

Many scriptures have been twisted from the Bible to create obligation and guilt for the purpose of manipulation. "Wives submit!" is the favorite scripture of the male controller. This becomes his justification to force his wife into his every desire. This scripture does not, however, override every other scripture in the Bible. It does not void out, *"Husbands love your wives even as Christ loved the church."* Ephesians 5:25. It does not void out that all things should be done in love, that nothing should be done in selfishness. There are hundreds of scriptures that must be violated in order for this submission scripture to become the pivotal point of the marriage.

Real love never oversteps certain bounds. It never violates another person's will. It doesn't demand, it compels. It never takes another person's freedom of choice from them. It is never given with *me* in mind. It is always given with *you* in mind.

8

WHAT IS LOVE?

This seems like such a mystical question. It is only mystical, however, because we have refused to look to the Author of love to find its meaning. We have looked in all the wrong places only to find all the wrong meanings. God is the Author of love because He is Love. *"And we have known and believed the love that God hath to us. God is love; and he that dwelleth in love dwelleth in God, and God in him."* 1 John 4:16.

Only the love that God describes can produce the kind of results that we hope for. To the degree we move away from God's definition of love, we will experience pain and difficulty in our relationships.

The King James version of the Bible describes God's *agape* love as follows: *"Charity suffereth long, and is kind; charity envieth not; charity vaunteth not itself, is not puffed up, Doth not behave itself unseemly, seeketh not her own, is not easily provoked, thinketh no evil; Rejoiceth not in iniquity, but rejoiceth in the truth; Beareth all things, believeth all things, hopeth all things, endureth all things. Charity never faileth."* 1 Corinthians 13:4-8

In the ***Prayer Organizer***[1] I have expanded the definition of these words used in 1 Corinthians 13.

Love is patient, it does not become angry. It endures under pressure. The codependent, toxic lover is never patient. They need for you to respond to their needs at their every whim. True love, however, is longsuffering. It allows you the time to work through your problems. It is not reactionary. *Love is kind.* Kindness is essential to love. The toxic love user is harsh and hard, not gentle and well behaved. It views kindness as something that is given as a reward. When you please the codependent he will reward you with kindness. When you fail to please, kindness is withdrawn. With God's love, kindness is a frame of mind. It is an attitude and a manner in which you treat all people because of the value you have for them.

Love does not envy. It is not jealous or possessive. It does not seek to control. It gives room for freedom of expression apart from self. In toxic love, jealousy is offered as proof of love. "I love you so much I just can't stand to see you talking to someone else." What this really means is, "I don't want you to have any friends, I don't want you to have any fulfillment, apart from me." Otherwise you might realize that you could be happy without me. My security is not in the fact that you are receiving true love from me, it is that you are not allowed to experience anything good from anyone else. I can't allow you to have satisfaction apart from me.

Love does not boast. In other words, it is not obsessed with drawing attention to self by bragging or exaggerating about self and personal accomplishment. The braggart builds a false sense of security through vain deceit. He has an extreme overestimation of self. He tries to convince others of how great he is as a way to earn a certain response. He is very anxious to impress. After all, the world revolves around his need to be loved.

The love of God is not proud. The proud person is an unteachable fool who delights in airing his own opinions. He can't admit that he needs to be taught. To do so would be tantamount to admitting weakness. And in his mind, people will only love and respect him when he is right; therefore, he can't admit to being wrong. The proud person is always surrounded by strife and conflict. *"Only by pride cometh contention: but with the well advised is wisdom"* Proverbs 13:10

The proud person is driven by the need to be right. Really, he doesn't need to be right as much as he needs for everyone to perceive him as being right. Many of the conflicts in his life are brought about by his need to prove himself right.

The love of God is not rude. It has good manners. It is able to show proper respect. The need to dominate is always rude. It has no real value for the other person or their feelings. Regardless of how cordial and diplomatic, in the end your feelings don't matter. When we walk in the love of God, we have a value for good manners. We are interested in protecting the feelings and worth of other people. Our style of communication and our treatment of others always reflects worth and value for them as a person.

One of the greatest aspects of God's love working in our life is that it is not self-seeking. Self-centeredness is always at the heart of every sinful, negative action in our life. True love does not use others for personal gratification. Instead, it seeks to give of self for the benefit of others. The self-centered individual has one primary question about all of his effort, "What do I get out of this?" This is always his personal and often secret motivation. The self-seeking person is always working an agenda.

God's love is not easily angered. It is not explosive. It doesn't take things too personal. The codependent, on the other hand, is always angered when things are out of his control. When people do not respond the way he wants, when he is threatened or when he is embarrassed, he becomes explosive. You find that you must always guard your words and actions when he is around. You feel like you are "walking on egg shells."

"I'm sorry I blew up on you like that," or "I didn't mean to hurt you, I just love you so much I get a little crazy sometimes." The codependent justifies his extreme, unacceptable behavior as some expression of extreme, precious love that is so great, it just sometimes loses control. The passive codependent tries to believe it is love. "Sure he gets mad and beats me up sometimes, or sure he embarrasses me in public, but he loves me so much and I do such stupid things."

God's love keeps no record of wrongs. It does not dwell on past hurts nor does it use the past as a way to manipulate. Love doesn't use past failures as a way to create guilt. It is anxious to forgive and forget. Because the codependent views himself as a victim, he is ever aware of past hurts. He seems to have difficulty leaving the past behind.

God's love does not rejoice in evil. It does not find satisfaction when others are found to be wrong. It does not use the faults of others as a way to justify self. The codependent often delights in seeing the faults of others. He seems to look for the dirt. This is a pathway to empowerment over the one found in fault. This justifies his wrong actions.

Instead of looking for fault, true love rejoices with the truth. True love is always happy when others find and live in the truth. It delights when others come into a healthy trust for God. Because our church builds strong self-worth, I have often lost members to this cause. If someone is married to a controller and they begin to discover who they are in Jesus, this threatens the empowerment of the controller. He will leave the church if he sees that it is causing him to lose control of his mate. He doesn't rejoice with the truth.

Love protects. This doesn't happen in an unhealthy way. There is a difference between protecting and defending. Love protects not only by encouragement and acceptance, but also by correction when necessary. Love doesn't try to isolate people from the pain they create for themselves, it simply accepts the person while they are in those situations. Love realizes that people must face the consequences of their actions, otherwise they will never grow and become responsible. But love also realizes that a persons self-worth needs to be protected, even when they must be confronted. Therefore, love doesn't attack the individual, it merely addresses the actions of the individual.

Love always trusts. Many think this is a naive, blind trust, but this is not the case. Love desires to trust. It looks for the best in others, but it yields to the Biblical admonition that says, "*A righteous man is cautious in friendships.*" Proverbs 12:26 NIV. Some people who are afraid of love, think it will make them vulnerable to manipulation. They think that love is being a doormat. Much the contrary, it takes great strength to walk in love. A person who loves never allows another to define love. I will not love you the way you say love is, I will love you the way God says love is.

Love is given; trust is earned. We can only trust a person to the degree that we know them and their track record. If they are not worthy of trust, it should not be given. Yet love always allows one to have the opportunity to establish a new track record.

Love always hopes. Hope is the expectation of good. When we love someone, we never lose hope of what God can do in their life. People tend to live up to our expectations. To some degree our expectations forge their future. If we expect the worst, we treat them accordingly. Our treatment of them can bring out the worst. It becomes a self-fulfilling prophecy. When we have hope, we treat the person differently. After all, our hope is not in that person, our hope is in God who, when given the opportunity, can work mightily in anyone's life.

Love never fails. Many things will fail to work, but the one thing that will never fail or cease to be effective is love. If anything has the potential to effect a person's life, love does. When people will not respond to miraculous gifts like tongues and prophecy, they will still respond to love. When we can't find the knowledge to answer their questions and meet their needs, love can still work. Love can effect a person beyond the realm of knowledge.

Agape love may lose affection, it may lose erotic desire, but it is always willing to provide the kind of love God gives.

[1] *The Prayer Organizer*, Dr. James B. Richards
Impact Ministries, Huntsville, Alabama

9

LOVE ON DIFFERENT LEVELS

Our world around us is basically a response to our present style of communication. We had no choice what kind of family we would be born into. We didn't have a choice about our siblings. No one asked us what school we would go to. It was unfortunate that we sat next to the most sarcastic, cruel, hurtful boy in school. There are things about our appearance that may be less than desirable. There have been many things in life over which we had no choice. But today, we have choices.

Today, I can choose how I will relate to my past and my present, all of which will determine my future. I have the freedom of response. I can respond to the things over which I had no control in a way that keeps my present life out of control. Or, I can take control of my attitudes and actions and I can experience change in my world.

My world is a reactionary world; it reacts to me. Every minute of everyday I stimulate reactions in the people around me, which means I am in control of my life. But I don't want to be in control of my life, I want to be in control of your life. The codependent puts forth every manner of vain effort to control the people around him, with little effort put forth in the area of self-control.

Proverbs 25:28 in the NIV says, "*Like a city whose walls are broken down is a man who lacks*

self control." In those days, a city without walls
didn't stand a chance against destruction.
Likewise, pain and destruction are imminent for
the person who has no self-control. It cannot be
avoided. Why? Because the codependent is the
creator of his pain. He didn't create his pain and
suffering as a child, he did not create his pain in
those areas over which he had no control, but today
he is creating his pain because he refuses to control
the one area that he can control, himself.

Codependent Christians are always focused
on how everyone else should be treating them. You
should walk in love; you should be kind to me; you
should understand my unique problems; you. . .you.
. .you. The moment you ask, "Well, what about
you?" Their typical response is, "You're judging me!
You're violating my boundaries, you're in my space,
you're trying to control me."

Like it or not, fair or unfair, we cannot expect
the people around us to be perfect. They have
hurts, pains and a past just like we do. What we
can certainly expect is that the people around us
will react to our actions. If we sow bad seed, we'll
reap a bad crop.

One of the most misquoted passages in the
Bible is Luke 6:38, "*Give, and it shall be given unto
you; good measure, pressed down, and shaken
together, and running over, shall men give into your
bosom. For with the same measure that ye mete
withal it shall be measured to you again.*" This
passage has nothing to do with money. This is
talking about the way we treat people. If you give
judgment, you'll reap ten times as much judgment.
If you give condemnation, you'll reap ten times as
much condemnation.

I had a lady come to me complaining that I

could not possibly understand her problem, because I always had friends. When I told her some things she could do to have friends, she said it was just impossible. "I don't have the money to feed people like you do. I can't have people into my home. I can't, I cant, I can't."

I explained, "Many times Brenda and I will feed needy people when we don't have any food left for us to eat. We have people in our home to help them, not buy their friendship. We are reaping what we are sowing; you are reaping what you are sowing."

Jesus warned that it would be this way. A warped Christian community has interpreted the passages about sowing and reaping into something that God was doing to you. Jesus said *"Men will heap unto your bosom."* This is the reaction of people to you.

Agape love is your response to God. The ability to walk in kindness, patience and the other qualities of 1 Corinthians 13 is the result of what is happening between you and God. When one believes and accepts the unconditional love of God, it becomes very difficult to stay bitter and angry. 1 John 4:8 says, *"He that loveth not, knoweth not God."* The word *knoweth* is a word that means to know experientially. In other words, the one who is not walking in love is simply not experiencing love at this moment.

When we believe the love of God, we can know (experience) the love of God. When we experience the love of God, our response will be to walk in love. By continually making ourselves aware of the hurts of the past, we respond to those hurts in a negative destructive way. If we were to begin making ourselves aware of the love of God, we would respond to His love. Whatever we choose to hold in our thoughts is what we choose to experience. What we experience is what determines the way we relate to the world around us.

Brotherly love, *phileo,* is a response to the way someone treats you. When we relate to others with the agape love of God, they respond to us in brotherly love. We reap what we sow. There will be some who are so dysfunctional they cannot respond to us properly, but that is not our problem. As a whole, we will reap the love that we are sowing.

In our marriages, we want *eros,* erotic love. We want to have a passionate relationship with our mate. We want the affection and excitement that we had in the beginning. If we treated one another the way we did then, we would still have all those feelings. That passion was a response to the way we were treating one another at that time.

When we found our mate, we treated them as the pearl of great price, they were precious to us. It showed in the way we treated them. But somewhere along the way, self-centeredness crept in and we changed. Maybe one day they disappointed us. Or, maybe we just said, "Well the chase is over, she's mine, now I can be myself." Regardless of the reason, they are no longer our pearl of great price and we change the way we treat them. They respond to us in like manner.

All of life is a series of choices that stimulate people around us in a positive or negative way. If I treat people good just for the desired result, that will be little more than manipulation. It will be something I will stop when I don't get what I want. But when we focus on and think about the love of God, we will begin to experience that love and we will demonstrate what we are experiencing. When the people around us experience the love of God through us, they will be more likely to respond in a loving manner. When we can give our spouse agape love, it creates phileo, friendship love.

Love can be experienced on all these different levels, but it must start with a choice to focus on and experience God's perfect love. As we experience that love, it matters little how those around us respond. As a whole, however, they will respond with all the different levels of love.

Therefore, the world around me is reacting to the way I relate to it. I can sow love, kindness, patience, or control, manipulation, and selfishness. Whatever I give I can be sure the world will give it back to me . . . "pressed down, shaken together, and running over."

10

DESTRUCTIVE ASSOCIATIONS

What would ever make a person expose themselves to painful situations over and again? How could someone allow themselves to be humiliated and yet feel the need to stay? Why does a person feel the need to cling to a destructive relationship? These questions could be answered a thousand different ways and obviously every situation is somewhat different. We may never know the intricate reasoning behind a person's destructive actions, but there are some things that we do know.

We know that God created every person to be a social, emotional, relationship-oriented being. We know that people's physical and mental health thrives in a healthy, loving environment. We know that everyone has, at the seat of his being, the need to be loved and accepted. We know that every desire a man has comes from a God-given root, however perverted and twisted it may have become.

Our distorted concepts of love are a major factor in the codependent cycle. We all want to be loved. The problem is often found in our understanding of love. Because we have not accepted God's definition of love, we have, by default, accepted some other definition. We have established certain psychological associations with love. However dysfunctional our concept of love is will play a role in determining how dysfunctional we will become to get the need for love met in our life.

For example, if a child grows up in a physically abusive home, she may accept a distorted concept of love. Let's say her father beats her and convinces her that it is an act of love. Now she considers beating to be a normal part of what you have to go through to be loved. She may even go as far to think that if a man loves her he must beat her. Her need to be loved will draw her into and cause her to remain in an abusive situation. In her mind, it is the only way to feel loved.

Regardless of what is working at the psychological level, there is one thing that is sure. She is sure that she wants to be loved. And that need for love will cause her to endure nearly any kind of abuse. If she accepted God's definition of love, she would know that she is not really experiencing love. She could make a rational decision to reject that kind of treatment and pursue real love.

Long before she had the mental and emotional maturity to make rational choices, she had someone program into her mind that love was expressed through beatings. At a subconscious level, far below her ability to reason, she has established a destructive association. It is not rational. It makes no sense at all. It is painful, but it is what she believes to be the pathway to find love.

The same thing can happen with sexual situations. It has long been my observation that many sexually abused children become very promiscuous. While there are many factors involved in this scenario, the concept of love plays a major role. I have seen women and men do things that bring them so much pain and shame that they would become suicidal. As soon as they "pulled themselves together," they would be right back doing the same destructive things. Why? A destructive association. Let's say someone is sexually molesting a child. At a time of great emotion, the offender is telling her it is because he loves her. Any information that is received during times of strong emotion creates an association. Or as the Bible says, "*It is written on the table of the heart.*" Once something is written on our heart, it becomes second nature. It becomes a part of our subconscious beliefs. It directs our decisions without conscious thought.

Even though promiscuity is a degrading, shameful experience for her, it is the pathway to being loved. She is convinced that sex and love are the same thing. Or, at least, sex makes her feel loved. Until she breaks that destructive association, she will continue to degrade herself with the thing she hates, searching for the thing she needs. . .love.

It has been said that most of our basic beliefs are established by the time we are five years old. We have associations, beliefs and concepts that were established at such an early age, we don't know where they came from, yet they are driving our life today. Think of it, most of my destructive behavior is because I am using the rational of a three year old. These beliefs were developed when I was a child. No wonder the codependent often seems to make such infantile decisions.

The world, especially the church world, has failed to understand the need for love and the dynamics of the love of God. Think of it, we all need to know we are loved. This will be the basis for our self-worth. The worth we place on ourselves is directly proportional to the worth we perceive that others have for us. Our level of self-worth determines every decision we will ever make in this life.

A person with low self-worth does not feel worthy of love. He does not believe he can be loved. As a child, I spent most of my days with my grandmother, while my mother worked. My grandmother had deep emotional problems. They were not obvious to most people. They only became obvious in close quarters.

My grandmother convinced me that I was unlovable. Most of my life that's what I believed. I would destroy every relationship I was in. As soon as the relationship began to look like love, I would sabotage it. I was operating on a belief that was established in my heart before I was five years old. I didn't know where it came from. I never even realized why I did the things I did until later in life.

This meant that every relationship ended in pain, yet my need to be loved drove me to keep getting into relationships. My need to be loved was stronger than my dread of the pain, so I repeated the cycle for years.

We all want to be loved and accepted. God made that to be a part of our emotional make up. But, He intended for us to look to Him to find that love. In so doing, we would have complete emotional stability and peace. When we saw the great worth He had for us, we would have an incredible sense of self-worth.

Instead of the church proclaiming the love of God, we have proclaimed the wrath of God. Because we do not believe the goodness of God brings us to repentance, we have determined good and evil for ourselves. We try to bring people to God through fear instead of through love. We try to manipulate instead of compel. We do not preach the gospel (good news), we preach bad news.

Think of it! We tell people that if they don't get saved, God hates them and has no value for them. Then when they do get saved we tell them that if they don't live right, God still has no value for them. This means people have to look somewhere else to find the love that God desires to give them. We push people away from God because we do not believe or proclaim the love of God.

Yet the need still exists. The need to experience perfect, unwavering love. We have to have it from someone. The problem is, there is no one on this earth that can meet that need. Our only source for perfect love has been so slandered that we also have destructive associations about God.

When bad things happen to people, we say it's God. When good things happen to people we say it is luck. If a tornado destroyed five houses in a row and skipped one, we would say the five destroyed was an act of God, but "Man, wasn't that sixth guy lucky." A dread has been put in the hearts of many children about God. When they are grown, they still have this infantile belief that God is a source of pain and rejection.

One of the most difficult tasks I face as a minister is getting grown people to believe God is a good God. They will read the New Testament. They intellectually acknowledge that Jesus represented God, yet there is still a mentality of a good Jesus and a bad God. This destructive association will drive a person away from the only source of complete love and acceptance to a lifetime of pain and rejection.

Negative, destructive associations must be identified and eradicated. We must write the truth about God on our hearts. We must establish our hearts on the Biblical concepts of love.

This will not happen automatically or accidentally. I invest in my life daily by reading, praying, and meditating on the Word of God. I have written new things on my heart. Those old associations have been replaced. My every thought of God, life, and love is positive and rewarding.

You, too, can establish new, life-giving associations. Find and use a method that works for you.

11

VICTIM'S MENTALITY

At the seat of all abuse problems you find a person who is inept in personal relationship skills. His emotional perceptions create inter-personal conflicts that make it impossible to have healthy relationships. This vacuum in his life from unfulfilled relationships can lead to all types of addictions. As I have often heard it said, "Codependency is the mother of all addictions." Out of a God-given need for meaningful relationships we develop all manner of problems. The need for love and acceptance dominates our emotions. The need for meaningful socialization drives us, but destructive attitudes and behaviors make it nearly impossible to have good relations, so we try to fill the void in very destructive ways.

Instead of realizing how one's behavior is negatively affecting his every relationship, the codependent assumes that he is being victimized by others. He often feels that the entire world is against him. He feels that he is helpless against those who seek to hurt him. He believes himself to be a victim.

The person with the victim's attitude feels that he is powerless to do anything about his life, or he feels that others unfairly inflict pain upon him. It almost seems as if the world had a secret meeting and did not invite him. In this meeting, they all agreed to make him miserable. Regardless of which way the victim's mentality "tilts," it basically concludes that he is in no way responsible for how others react to him. Nor does he feel he could do anything about it. The Bible says, *"A fool's lips enter into contention, and his mouth calleth for strokes."* Proverbs 18:6. In other words, the way one talks creates contention, which leads to pain or punishment. The victim only focuses on what others are doing to hurt him. He cannot allow himself to focus on what he is doing to create these types of responses.

People in prison are outraged at how unfair the system is treating them. They consider themselves to be victims of the system, yet they never consider that they took someone's life or they stole or they broke laws that put them in the position they are in. The codependent victim focuses all of his attention on others with no consideration for his personal actions.

Our society has nourished the codependent victim's mentality by focusing the blame on who has hurt us and caused our pain, instead of what we can do to overcome the pain. Many times, I counsel with people who have gone through years of therapy, spent thousands of dollars and all they have done is determined who they would blame for their problems. The victim always has someone to blame. Placing blame gives a false sense of justification for our unacceptable behavior. As long as I have someone to blame, I'm okay, right? No! You're not okay, you still have no friends, no meaningful relationships and no self-worth. Finding someone to blame has never healed one emotional conflict. Learning how to live responsibly in society is the only thing that will change your world.

I must realize that my dysfunctional behavior creates reactions in others. I can idealistically talk about how they should love me, accept me, and respond to me, but that is mere idealism. If I want friends, I must learn to be a friend. (Proverbs 18:24) People respond negatively to me, just like I respond negatively to them. I want them to overlook and justify my dysfunction, but I will not overlook theirs. God created me to be a social being, I must learn to function as one.

The government cannot pass laws that make others relate to me properly, nor should I expect that. The preacher can't make the church love me. No one else can create the kind of responses that I desire from others. Only I have the power to do that. I will live in the world that I create by my words and actions and I must be happy with it. It's all I'll ever have.

Proverbs 18:20-21 in the Amplified Bible[1] says it this way, *"A man's moral self shall be filled with the fruit of his mouth, and with the consequences of his words he must be satisfied whether good or evil. Death and life are in the power of the tongue, and they who indulge it shall eat the fruit of it for death or life."* On the street they say, "You better make those words sweet when they come out, because you'll eventually have to eat them."

"A fool's mouth is his destruction, and his lips are the snare of his soul." Proverbs 18:7. The codependent creates strife and destruction with his words and actions. He enters into the realm of sowing and reaping. Sometimes he actually tries to be extreme, to force others into giving him the unconditional love that only God can give. It is as if

he wants the world to prove to him that he is loved. Yet when he has to experience the negative consequences of his actions, he feels that he is being victimized.

There is a law of sowing and reaping that continues every day, whether we believe it or not. We reap the results of our actions daily. The way people treat us today is a product of how we treated them yesterday. The religious teaching concerning sowing and reaping has led us to believe that when we do something it creates a reaction from God. So we believe the pain in our life is some reaction from an angry God. Not true! God loves us unconditionally, yet we still must live with the consequences of our actions.

Sowing and reaping happens on the horizontal plane, not the vertical. God is always good to me, but the people that I hurt and insult are not. They react to my unacceptable behavior. They react to my lack of tact. They react to my harsh words. They do things that hurt me in response to my actions. But that does not make me a victim.

I once had a preacher friend who made bizarre statements from the pulpit. When he would do that, people would respond negatively. He felt that there was some great value in shocking people, but when people would respond to him in a way that he did not appreciate, he felt he was the victim. He felt that people were doing him wrong. He was quick to point out how unfair others were to him, but never accepted his part in creating the problem. More than once I tried to warn him, "If you're going to take that approach to ministry, you'll have to live with the consequences."

It's like a girl who attended my church. She would come to church with her hair dyed green and would wear strange clothes. Sometimes she would have on no shoes and two very different colors of socks. She would complain that she didn't feel close to anyone. She did not want to accept that just as she had the freedom to dress how she desired, they had the freedom to respond how they desired. When you violate culture or what is socially acceptable; right or wrong, you better be ready to live with the response.

The codependent is quick to point out how everyone else should have the love of God. With no consideration that they are not walking in love. I have often had people come to me and complain that they had no friends. They complained that no one loved them, "If these people really were Christians, they would treat me right." More than once, all I could say is, "You're not a very friendly person. No one is obligated to be your friend. If you want friends, you've got to change."

I had a young man in my church that had come out of a homosexual background. He did very well for a while. Later, he began to dress effeminate and wear his hair in an effeminate way. He came to me complaining that people thought he was still gay. He also complained that gay men were "hitting on him." All I could say was, "You're dressing like you're gay; you're acting like you're gay. If you don't want society to think you're gay, you must make the changes that are necessary." He complained, "Well, they have no right to think I'm gay just because of the way I dress!" And I responded, "You're right, but you have no right to expect them to think anything other than what you show them."

I have seen a common denominator when dealing with people from a homosexual background:

the victim's mentality. A homosexual lifestyle defies nature, it defies God, and it defies society. It is a life of extreme behavior. When society doesn't respond to the homosexual the way he/she desires, he/she feels victimized. This seems to be the attitude that is carried forward into their new life that ultimately causes them to fall. I have seen very few ex-homosexuals fall simply because they wanted to have a homosexual lifestyle; it is usually the victim's mentality that causes them to have offense against the church. They still have a tendency in daily life to yield to the bizarre or flamboyant and feel victimized by the reactions of others.

I am not saying society is right in all of their responses. I am saying, however, that we should count the cost before we act and speak. Are we really ready to accept society's reaction to our behavior? Do we really understand how it will affect us to lose the acceptance of our friends?

"The slothful man saith, There is a lion without, I shall be slain in the streets." Proverbs 22:13. Sloth is an attitude. It is an attitude that produces laziness. It is an attitude that discourages responsibility. The person with this attitude is paralyzed. He feels that he cannot go out and pursue life because there is danger out there for him. He fears that he will be victimized. He feels that he has no control over what will happen to him. He has no sense of responsibility.

The slothful man chooses to live an irresponsible lifestyle and blame others for their reactions. His low self-worth fears that there would be more pain in change than there would be in rejection. So he spends his life trying to force others to respond the way he wants. In the end, it is just another sad attempt at control.

[1]   *The Amplified Bible,* Zondervan Bible Publishers, Grand Rapids, MI

12

Blame vs. Responsibility

One of the crippling paradigms of the codependent lies in his inability to distinguish the difference between guilt and blame. This perceptional problem paralyzes an individual in a place of irreconcilable conflict. It makes every trap a snare from which there is no escape. Every attempt to free himself only causes the jaws of destruction to grip tighter.

Blame points to the past. It points to the wrong. Blame determines who should be punished or penalized. Blame has absolutely no value in solving the problem. It actually becomes part of justifying the problem. The entire "blame mentality" seems to think the one who is to blame is the one who is responsible. In other words, "You broke it, you fix it."

Responsibility, on the other hand, determines who will be responsible to solve the problem. You can blame who you want to for the problem, but who will assume responsibility to solve the problem? Responsibility looks to the future. It looks to the cure. It assumes the obligation to find the cure.

There are few cases where the one who is to blame for the damage will be the one who will assume responsibility for the recovery. You may have been victimized, but that doesn't mean you are a perpetual victim. A victim is helpless to do anything. We are not helpless.

Someone else may have caused me to be in the pain I am in. I may have caused myself to be in the pain I am in. But who caused it does not matter, I am the only one who can do anything about it. If I surrender my responsibility, I have determined to live the rest of my life as a victim. I can only have freedom to the degree that I assume responsibility.

If the codependent confuses blame for the problem with the responsibility to solve the problem, his low self-esteem will not allow him to find the cure. The codependent already feels too guilty for too many things. He can't bear to lay another brick to the load. To accept responsibility would be more additional pain than he could bear, so he seeks to find relief by searching out a source to blame.

The codependent does not realize the unconditional love of God. He does not know that God can love him even if he is the source of the problem. Not only would God continue to love him, God would deliver him. The codependent must justify himself before God and man. He must be proven right. He cannot bear being wrong. And there is, of course, the person who swings to the other extreme and assumes the blame for every thing. This is a defense mechanism that is used to keep from dealing with problems on any serious level.

The Bibles says in Ephesians 6:15 that one should have, "*Your feet shod with the preparation of the gospel of peace.*" Our feet provide our foundation, our stability. Thayer's Lexicon translates preparation as "a firm foundation that comes from a readiness of mind."[1] In hand to hand combat, it is essential that one never lose balance. One must have a readiness of mind and be able to respond to an attack that comes from any direction without losing his footing.

In the martial arts, one is taught to move in a circular motion away from every attack in a way that not only maintains your balance, but it throws the opponent off balance. To do this requires a readiness of mind. One must respond instinctively and instantly. It also requires the knowledge of how to respond. The same is true emotionally.

When guilt, condemnation, and shame hit me, I must maintain my footing in the gospel of peace.[2] My first response cannot be to blame shift. While I am looking for someone to blame, I am being destroyed. My first response should always be, "No matter what is happening, God is at peace with me through the Lord Jesus Christ. God is not doing this to me." This causes me to keep my footing, both emotionally and spiritually.

Even if I am the problem, I can face it and admit it if I know that I will not lose the love and acceptance of God. Being wrong is not a big issue for the one who is established in peace. Unfortunately, religion has tried to make everything revolve around being right. In Christianity, however, everything revolves around the finished work of Jesus. The religious codependent must prove himself right in order to maintain his footing (his standing with God), therefore, he can rarely ever work through any major problems. From his perspective, being wrong would bring rejection and punishment from God. So all of his emotional energy revolves around trying to prove he is right.

If I know there is peace between me and God

because of Jesus, I have the freedom to deal with getting healed and getting free. We can figure out whose fault it is later. When someone wrongs me, I don't consider myself a victim; I can do something about it. I have a God who will never leave me, never forsake me, and never fail me.

But it's not fair. If it's not my fault, why do I have to be the one to do something about it? Who said life was fair? It's not! The reason I must do something about what is affecting my life is because I am the only one who can.

I once read an amusing story about a man walking down the beach. A seagull flew over and "pooped" on his nose. He became so angry at the seagull. He reasoned within himself, "That seagull did this to me and he's going to have to come back and get this off of me!" When he returns to his group of friends they are all repulsed. "What is that smell. Stay away from me!" they all shouted. Then they ran away from him. He became even more angry at the seagull, "Look what you've done to me," the man cried. "You come back right now and get this off of me."

When he goes home that night he wants to be intimate with his wife. She immediately kicks him out of bed and demands that he go wash his face. He lies on the couch lonely and rejected, contemplating how the seagull was ruining his life. His friends had run away from him, his wife had rejected him and he didn't do anything. All he could think was, "It's not my fault!"

When he goes to work the next day, people quickly go to the other side of the room to avoid him. The odor has become unbearable. The man had stopped bathing, because if he bathed he might remove the poop from his nose, then the seagull would have gotten by with his unfair treatment. Finally, his boss called him in and said, "None of the clients want to do business with you. None of the coworkers can stand to be in the same room with you. Either you wash that poop off of your nose or you're fired." The man's response was, "How unfair can you get? Why are you all persecuting me? I didn't do anything. I didn't put this on my nose, I shouldn't be the one to have to wash it off."

So now he sits alone under an overpass, victimized by the world. And everyday he looks out at the sky, because he knows who is to blame. And one day that rotten seagull will have to come and clean up his nose.[3]

This story seems so utterly foolish, yet I have seen many marriages end in divorce around this kind of logic. "He is the one who caused the problem, I'm not going to do anything about it." Millions of people go through pain everyday, feeling that someone else should come and fix the pain they inflicted. The truth is, it will never happen. If you want to be free from the past, quit living for the past. The past has no power to affect your life today beyond the significance that you attach to it or your unwillingness to change.

Maybe you didn't do it, but I'm sure that if it is affecting you, you can do something about it!

[1] *Thayer Greek-English Lexicon of the New Testament*, Baker Book House, Grand Rapids, MI

[2] *The Gospel of Peace*, Dr. James B. Richards, Impact Ministries, Huntsville, Alabama

[3] Adapted from a story in *Foundations of Intercession*, Wes Daughenbaugh, Gospel Net Ministries, Omaha, NE

13

DESTRUCTIVE EXPECTATIONS

The codependent has unrealistic expectations of people, circumstances, and of life in general. Because he is looking to others to meet the needs that can only be met through a meaningful relationship with God, every relationship becomes a disappointment. No one or nothing lives up to the expectations of the codependent.

There are probably few attitudes that are as mean and hurtful as the expectations of the codependent.[1] Because we expect things of others, we enter every relationship poised to reject the other person. We do not get to know someone and allow the relationship to develop. We go in expecting them to meet certain needs. Before we ever know them, before we have ever given them an opportunity, we have rejected them because they did not meet our expectations.

The codependent misses out on much of life and its opportunities. Every person we meet, every relationship, every circumstance holds new opportunities to learn and grow. We are given the opportunity to meet different kinds of people in different settings. We have the opportunity to have friendships on every different level. Each of these friendships has the potential to develop our relationship skills and prepare us for a life of happiness. But the codependent will never experience most of these joys of life. He is too busy attempting to find the person or situation that will meet his need, thereby, he never develops the relationship skills needed to have the meaningful involvement he desires.

One can never truly know the person upon whom you have imposed your expectations. We cheat ourselves out of the opportunity to grow and develop character, because we expect everyone to conform to our expectations instead of us yielding enough to have a variety of friendships.

The codependent thinks the opportunity for happiness simply never comes his way. Sadly, he has the same opportunities as everyone else in life. He simply does not see them because he rejects everything and everyone who does not fit into his paradigm.

The codependent thinks he knows what will make him happy. Therefore, he develops a type of selective reasoning. He defines a friend as "this kind of person." So, if you're not "this kind of person," he doesn't give you a chance. The irony is "this kind of person" has never made the codependent happy. Because he is convinced, however, that this is what he needs, he searches for it relentlessly. Rejecting all other possibilities.

The codependent says, "I need you to make me happy. I expect things of you so that I will be happy. The entire purpose of this relationship was so you could make me happy. If you fail to meet these needs, I will reject you." Our expectations of others causes us to reject them before we even know them.

One of the sickest motivations for a relationship is need. "I need you!" is the mating call of the codependent. In other words, "I have needs I expect you to meet. This relationship is all about me and my needs. I want you to live up to my expectations."

These expectations form the basis of the majority of inter-personal conflict for the codependent. It fuels his hurt and disappointment with life. It may be rare that anyone actually creates a real offense against the codependent, yet in his mind, it happens regularly. A codependent feels that people regularly and deliberately hurt him, but what he interprets as acts of aggression are really just those times when people fail to meet his expectations.

Jesus told a parable about a man who hired workers out of the market place. He hired some of them first thing in the morning and promised to give them "a penny," (a days wages). The man goes out about an hour later and hires more workers and offers them the same pay. He does this throughout the day and about the last hour of the day he hires even more. When he begins to pay the workers, he pays the ones he hired last. He gives them a full days pay. *"But when the first came, they supposed that they should have received more; and they likewise received every man a penny. And when they had received it, they murmured against the good man of the house."* Matthew 20:10-11.

The key word in this passage is *supposed,* they *supposed* they would receive more. They were not promised more; they expected more. They had a logic they worked from, but their logic was wrong. The man paid them just what he had committed. Although he had done them no wrong, they became offended. Their offense, however, did not come from the person, it came from their expectations.

What this story doesn't tell is how these

codependent workers went forth and told this story to their friends. "It was so unfair. We worked all day long in the sun. We did ten times as much work as those other guys and he only paid us one hours wages." By the time it's over, people are afraid to come and work for the man because they are afraid he will cheat them out of their pay.

Because control is the goal of the codependent, it is impossible for the codependent to stay in a relationship he cannot control. The codependent will despise a kind person if it is a person he can't control. People often tell me stories about some pastor who offended them. They may even have horror stories of how he controlled them. When we get to the root of the problem, the codependent is actually angry because he couldn't control the other person.

Jesus faced the false expectations of the people daily. It was not the things that Jesus did that caused the religious world to reject him as much as it was the things He didn't do. He didn't live up to their expectations, and true to the codependent code of ethics, when He failed to meet their expectations, they rejected Him and killed Him.

Listen to people in the Bible express their false expectations of what the Messiah would be like. The woman at the well said, "We know that when Christ comes, He will know all things." There was not one scripture in the Bible that said this. The Pharisees said, "*If you are the Christ show us a sign.*" Matthew 12:38. They had seen every sort of miracle, they just had not seen the one they wanted, more free food. In Jerusalem the Jews said, "We know where this man came from. When Christ comes no one will know where He comes from." The Bible was very clear about where Christ would come from and they only thought they knew where Jesus was from. Even the thief on the cross said, *"If you are the Christ come down from the cross."* Luke 23:39. Everyone had their expectations, but they didn't get them from what God had committed in the Scriptures.

God had promised a Messiah who would come the first time as a man who would suffer and die for their sins. That was not the kind of Messiah they needed. They needed a Messiah who would be a military leader and break the yoke of Rome from their necks. Like so many codependent people, what they thought they needed, and what they really needed were worlds apart.

In one situation, Jesus healed a crippled man. To experience such an act of kindness must have been overwhelming. I'm sure the man reasoned, "I've got sin in my life, I have problems, but Jesus healed me anyway. I bet he doesn't even care about the sin in my life." In the face of unbelievable mercy, the man reasoned until he reached an unrealistic expectation. John 5:14 says, *"Afterward Jesus findeth him in the temple, and said unto him, Behold, thou art made whole: sin no more, lest a worse thing come unto thee."*

This man's paradigm had just been broken. Although Jesus had healed him and shown him great mercy, He still wanted to deal with this sin issue. Jesus wasn't angry with him because of his sin, he was concerned. He knew how sin could effect the heart of this man. The man totally misinterpreted what this meant. In verses 15 and 16 it continues, *"The man departed, and told the Jews that it was Jesus, which had made him whole. And therefore did the Jews persecute Jesus, and sought to slay him, because he had done these things on the Sabbath day."*

A man who had just received healing now brought about the persecution that ultimately led to Jesus' crucifixion. Was any of this because Jesus had wronged him? No! It was all because Jesus failed to live up to the man's expectations. He believed he had been wronged. He probably went out and told people how critical and judgmental Jesus had been.

Jesus, like most preachers, was betrayed the most by some of the ones he helped the most. He, however, did not fall into the codependent leadership trap. He did not develop expectations of the people because of what He had done for them. He knew they were still people with problems.

The Bible explains a little about Satan's fall. Ezekiel 28:17 says, *"Thine heart was lifted up because of thy beauty, thou hast corrupted thy wisdom by reason of thy brightness: I will cast thee to the ground, I will lay thee before kings, that they may behold thee."* Satan corrupted his wisdom and reasoned his way into his fall. But his reasoning began with something that was real. In his case, it was his brightness and splendor.

The codependent may begin his reasoning at a point that is rational. Like Satan, however, we can reason beyond reality. Satan's reasoning was like adding one point to another point, to another point until he surpassed truth and reality. The men in the parable that Jesus taught, began with a reality. "Look, he paid those who worked one hour a full days wages." This was a reality.

From here they took a quantum leap and said, "He owes us more because we have worked all day." That was no longer reality. Reality could have been, "Possibly he will pay us more," or "We can ask him for more pay tomorrow." Any number of things would have kept them in reality. Instead, however, they created an expectation that they had no right to create. And instead of being thankful that they had the opportunity to work that day, they were offended and unthankful.

Instead of being thankful for what we do have, we are angry because of what we don't have. We put those around us under the pressure of living up to our expectations. We expect what was not promised. Sometimes we expect what is not possible. Through our expectations we become unthankful people who destroy meaningful relationships. The expectation of our friends is what destroys our relationships with them. The expectation of our mate is often what destroys our marriage. The expectation of my church will destroy my relationship with my church. My expectation of you makes me try to control you. In the end, the codependent will feel betrayed and offended. His expectations cause him to believe he has been wronged.

[1] *My Church My Family*, Dr. James B. Richards, Impact Ministries, Huntsville, Alabama

SECTION 2:
CODEPENDENCE
IN SOCIETY

SECTION 2:
INTRODUCTION

In order to properly understand how codependency has permeated so many areas of our thinking, it is essential that we identify the very subtle ways it has been introduced into every area of our lives. No one decided to make the entire world codependent, yet the very philosophies by which the world operates ultimately lead to codependency.

Greed and power can only function in a codependent society. Therefore, the attempt to set up a world economy simultaneously calls for a codependent society. Marketing flourishes by making people feel they have a need. If people aren't made to feel needy, very little can be bought or sold.

What people once considered luxuries are now considered to be essential needs. Happiness is sold by the advertisers, forming the thoughts and values of the young and old alike. The Bibles says in 1 John 2:15-16, *"Love not the world, neither the things that are in the world. If any man love the world, the love of the Father is not in him. For all that is in the world, the lust of the flesh, and the lust of the eyes, and the pride of life, is not of the Father, but is of the world."*

When a person longs for the things of the world, the love of the Father cannot find a place in him. When he is looking to the things of the world to meet the need that only God can meet, he can never really get the need met. Advertisers put the love of the world in the hearts of men. By so doing, they make the human race dependent on their merchandise for fulfillment.

In a recent news program about smoking, young teens said they were more influenced to smoke by advertising than by peer pressure. Strong associations about love, sex, happiness, and self-worth are made by coupling information with images. Everyone knows what they would "walk a mile for." Everyone knows what "tastes good like a cigarette should." We have had these images etched onto our minds.

All that the world has to offer meets the criteria for 1 John 2:16. It looks good, it feels good, and it makes me feel like somebody. I'm hooked! I need your stuff so I can feel good about me.

The concepts that are embraced by the world's economic system sound very much like the great whore in the book of Revelation. By them, the entire world is deceived. By them, wars are fought. By them, countries and their leaders rise and fall. The desire for a world economy is the one thing that has been able to unite the countries of the world into a false peace.

This section in no way deals fully with all the issues involved, nor does it attempt to be an authoritative source concerning this topic. It merely attempts to look at the basic areas that influence our thinking. (i.e. Family, Government, Education and Mental Health)

This thumbnail sketch will show how the basic philosophies that touch every life have been molded to effect our life paradigm, our sense of self-worth, our view of God, and to some degree, who we would look to for security. We are daily saturated with a constant barrage of information that is somewhat rational. Even when it is not rational, it is constant. As someone once said, "We'll believe a lie that we've heard all of our life before we'll believe the truth that we've only heard once." The constant message continually appears to be true.

This section is deliberately short. I do not desire to cause one to dive into the hopeless perils of the world system. I merely hope to open the readers eyes to the degree of the problem so he/she will fervently seek the solution. Unless we get real about the magnitude of the problem, we will never seriously deal with the problem.

The church is like the frog in the pot. If you were to drop him into boiling water, he would jump out and escape. But if you slowly turn up the heat, he will sit there until he is cooked. We've sat in the pot so long we don't realize that it is about to boil.

Be assured there is a solution. Solving this problem may not be as difficult as it seems. God has easy solutions for difficult situations. Don't lose hope or become overwhelmed as you read.

14

THE WORLD SYSTEM

All of my Christian life I have heard the stories and read the books that suggest a worldwide conspiracy. We know, in the end, there will be a one-world government. We know that it seems as if there is a monumental conspiracy, but the truth is, there doesn't have to be a conspiracy, as we know it, for the world to end up in chaos.

A conspiracy entered the earth at the garden when man became a sinner. Every human being born since Adam has been born a sinner. As a sinner, man has been afraid of God. He has hidden from Him. Man is afraid to trust God, therefore man is always looking somewhere other than God to get his needs met.

This was Satan's plan from the beginning. It became a conspiracy when he convinced Adam that he could be god of his own world and choose right and wrong based on his point of view rather than God's. From then until now, men and women have emerged that would show man the "way." At least, it was the way as far as the individual presenting it was concerned. He simply needed to get everyone to try his way so he could prove it was right.

The last generation of parents were raised under the philosophy that spanking children was unacceptable. They were taught by men who had opinions not facts, that striking children would cause them to be violent. They would come to accept violence as a way of life and it would cause aggression, etc.

This all seemed very reasonable and logical, and while it had never been proven, people accepted it in great numbers. But the biggest flaw was not that it had not been proven; the biggest flaw was that it contradicted the Bible. Man chose good and evil for himself, without regard to what God said.

I find it interesting to note that the children today who were raised by non-spanking parents have become the most violent, aggressive, out of control children history has ever seen. They thrive on violence, they seem to crave it. It seems that once again man's opinion was worthless. *(No doubt, there would have been great value in dealing with the issues of child abuse. Spanking and child abuse are, however, two different issues.)*

The Bible doesn't teach, as some suppose, that spanking is the answer for every disciplinary situation. Actually, we should be able to teach by compelling. We should instruct, lead, encourage and affirm our children in a way that draws them into responsible living. Yet some children are foolish. A fool is one who will not learn by instruction. Thus, the Bible says, *"Judgments are prepared for scorners, and stripes for the back of fools."* Proverbs 19:29.

When a child is so rebellious they will not learn from instruction, they must learn from consequence. If they do not learn from consequences, they will have no boundaries in life. They think they will always be able to do what they want and get by with it. They live their life out of control, as this generation of children are doing.

The more liberal politicians cram their liberal

concepts down the throat of American society, the worse that society becomes. Yet, they insist that if we could just have more of their ideas, everything would get better. But it doesn't. In fact, it gets worse. The farther we have moved from the basic values of the Bible, the more chaotic, violent and destructive society has become.

God is infinitely wiser than man. He has more experience in every area than man. He is the Creator; we are the creation. We are like the pot that attempts to instruct the potter. God gave us the wisdom we needed to maintain civil and social order. Our country, although not perfect, has thrived as a civilization by yielding, to some degree, to that wisdom. Although many things were done wrong, although there have been corrupt people hiding behind the Biblical principles, it has worked better than anything in any society has ever worked.

Why would man move away from something that God says would work? Time has proven it would work and everything they have tried has not worked. Simple! Man still wants to be god of his own world. Since man does not trust God, and since the church has persuaded the world that God is the source of all their pain, we have a modern day tower of Babel. We have a society seeking self-rule, freedom from the imagined tyranny of God.

Let me emphasize, I hold the church responsible for this turning away that has taken place in the world. The message of judgment and wrath has embittered the world against God. First, it created a concept of God that was unlovable. Then, it created a concept of God that could not be trusted. Finally, it contrived a character of God that rejected man. The god of the religious church is an immoral, unfaithful murderer.

Once the church turned the world against God, man now had the opportunity to create a world after his own image. That is the world system in which we now live. The Greek word *aion* which is translated as world, speaks of an age or era. It is more than an age in the sense of time, it is like an era of beliefs. We have entered into the era of man which will climax with the rise of 666, the totality of man. Man's era will be total chaos and anarchy. His ideas will reach the ultimate in failure and destruction. Apart from God and His wisdom, man's social order will fail at every point.

So there is a system at work in the world and it is based on codependency. It is the process of getting men to depend on anything and anyone other than God. Regardless of the conspiracies that may exist, people do not have to conspire for this to happen. All they have to do is stop trusting God. Stop depending on Him and you have a codependent society which epitomizes this world's system.

The Bible says in Romans 12:2, *"And be not conformed to this world: but be ye transformed by the renewing of your mind, that ye may prove what is that good, and acceptable, and perfect, will of God."* Man must renew his mind to be consistent with the Bible or else he will find himself conforming to this world system. The world's system is a codependent system. Even Christians who have not renewed their minds are a part of this system. They are saved, but are still in the world system.

The will of God is not hard and difficult as the church has proclaimed. Just the opposite, Jesus said, *"Come unto me, all ye that labour and are heavy laden, and I will give you rest. Take my yoke upon you, and learn of me; for I am meek and lowly in heart: and ye shall find rest unto your souls. For my yoke is easy, and my burden is light.*" Matthew 11:28-30. There is no place in the Bible that describes the will of God as hard. A renewed mind realizes that God's will is good, acceptable and perfect. It is a good thing.

The goodness of God is a reality that exists in the minds of people who have rejected their personal religious opinions and accepted God as Jesus presented Him. The fearful, unbelieving mind continues to draw back from God, leaving no choice but codependency. He must look to some source other than God to meet his deepest needs.

Because the world has accepted the religious view of God, they have determined that they want God out of every area of their life. They don't want their kids to pray to Him in school. They don't want their government to mention His name. They don't want His name on our currency. They want to stamp His memory from the face of the earth. To this day, people are censored, imprisoned, and sometimes killed for sharing the gospel.

But can you blame the world for taking this view? After all, they only know the concept of God that has been presented by an unbelieving church. For the most part, they have never heard the good news (gospel), all they have heard is bad news. I would not want to trust the god who was blamed for famine and draught. I would not want to know the god who was responsible for killing my children. I would not be friends with a god who always found fault with my every action. Nor does the world. They don't want the god we preach. He can't be trusted!

In light of the misinformation that has been proclaimed to the world, they have attempted to build a new Babylon, a society that exists without God. But everyone needs to believe in something. There is something in the very fabric of man that wants some type of "higher power." So man has created a god for man to depend on. He has built a system that calls for people to trust the government, trust the professionals, trust the educators, or trust in your riches. Pick the god of your choice, just don't trust the Living God!

Through advertising, education, and politics we have been led away from a simple trust in God. We choose to trust in the ideas of man. When a society turns away from God, there is no alternative but codependency. Man must have his deep emotional needs met in order to live. He must depend on someone to meet the needs that only God can meet.

Thus, we have an entire system, a way of life, and a society that rejects God. In His place, we have created a world's system, which does not work. It is not meeting the needs of society, but without God what else is there?

15

THE GOD OF GOVERNMENT

The progression toward codependency is not the fault of the church alone. The church simply gave man the reason not to trust God; from there the world has been able to do a wonderful job of offering other sources to trust. Every world leader has certain beliefs and intentions, which become imposed upon the population to some degree. Therefore, it is always essential for governments to brainwash the people in order for them to work their agenda with a minimum amount of resistance.

The farther a nation departs from the wisdom of God, the more that nation will plunge into irrational codependency. This is why communism has always had as its goal the abolishment of all religion. The communist leaders were shrewd enough to realize that you cannot create a totalitarian government in a godly society. They knew man had a need to yield himself to a higher power and that once God was removed from the society, man would look to the government as that higher power.

It has been amazing to see the atrocities committed against the people of the former Soviet Union, China, Germany and other nations. It is amazing that masses of people would stand idly by and allow the slaughter of other human beings. But they could not rise up against their source of security, the state. It is never long, however, before that which controls us by offering security, begins to control us through fear.

All the while the state is rejecting God and blaming Christianity of cruel oppression, they are forming another diabolical form of oppression. It seems that codependent people in government always attempt to create a society that empowers their group, their party, and themselves personally. This can only be done when people are disempowered and codependent. There need not be a formal conspiracy for this to happen; this is the world's system.

No one sits around and says, "How can we make the people codependent?" Instead, they say, "What do these people want?" Government leaders determine what it will take to buy your vote. They can count on the greed of the people. As the government meets needs, people begin to become dependent on government, thus you have a codependent society.

It has been said that men will quickly trade freedom for security. The United States has slowly proven that to be a reality. Every year, new laws are passed to protect the people that ultimately take more freedoms from them. The government that once existed to protect our freedom and our rights under the constitution, has now taken the role of meeting our needs.

One of the roles of the codependent controller is the "caretaker." The caretaker justifies violating your freedom in order to protect you from harm. But the more one person tries to protect another, the more he must violate his freedom of choice. The caretaker often assumes the superiority role and says, "These people are too ignorant to make the

right choices, we must make the choices for them."
He feels that his superiority gives him the right to
take away the rights of others.

Then there is the "savior mentality," which
goes a few steps beyond the caretaker. The
codependent savior not only wants to save people
from their mistakes, the savior wants to save them
from the consequences of their mistakes. This
mentality will keep a person from ever growing or
maturing. Fools only learn by paying the price for
their actions. This is what the Bible means when it
talks about stripes being for the back of the fool.
(Proverbs 19:29)

God is not trying to get us to inflict
punishment upon the fool, but He by no means
wants us to help the fool escape the results of his
actions. This assures that he will continue in the
same behavior. This reinforces his already faulty
belief that there are no consequences for his
actions. This is why most people that are released
from prison go back again. They have seldom been
made to bear the consequences of their actions.

Everyday, millions of dollars are awarded to
people who are considered to be victims. On the one
hand, companies pay millions of dollars in damages
for making their coffee too hot. There is never any
mention that an individual should use some
precautions and assume some responsibility. Never
mind his responsibility; he is a victim. At the same
time a murderer is acquitted because he is not
considered to be responsible for his actions. Think
of the irony, a murderer goes free without as much
as paying restitution, while a company that makes
their coffee too hot pays millions.

The codependent savior is willing to violate
the rights of the true victim in order to save the

criminal from his consequences. The codependent savior has no real help for the true victims, the hurting individual. They can only be perceived as a savior by someone who needs a savior. Thus you have the criminal justice system, designed for the criminal.

A person who has succeeded in life is somehow made to feel that he is the reason someone else is living in poverty. A man who works hard to provide a living for his family is penalized (taxed). Part of his earnings are forcibly taken and given to a man who is healthy, yet refuses to work. The citizens of our nation who cannot afford their own health care are made to pay for the health care of illegal aliens. There is more motivation for low income people to become dependent on the state than there is to earn a living. People who know how to work the system would be foolish to work a job.

There is a message that rings loud and clear in this nation: "If you are in lack, it is not your fault. If you've committed a crime, it is not your fault. If you are emotionally unstable, it is not your fault. Someone else is responsible to meet your needs." Therefore, our country, as a whole, has become a codependent nation. There is too much motivation to be irresponsible. But only irresponsible, codependent people need a codependent government.

Politicians run on a platform that says, "If you'll vote for me, I'll meet your needs." Every special interest group in America is promising to meet somebody's needs, but it will cost you some more of your freedoms. The most important freedom it will cost you is the freedom to trust God and experience His great goodness. It will cost you your self-worth. After the government supports you, you lose confidence in your ability to survive apart from the government. We slowly become slaves to the world's system.

True freedom is only found in trusting God. True self-worth is only known in a meaningful relationship with God. Awareness of significance is only experienced through living a life of significance. Unless God is our source, we will become the slave of the world's system.

God's economic structure, as presented in the Old Testament, provided for the poor. Every fifty years, all debts were cancelled. The poor were allowed to work the fields they did not own. There were many provisions for the poor, but not one of them made someone else responsible. God established a social order that would protect the innocent and deal with the guilty, yet man has become the god of his own world. He now "calls evil good and good evil." *"Woe unto them that call evil good, and good evil; that put darkness for light, and light for darkness; that put bitter for sweet, and sweet for bitter!"* Isaiah 5:20.

God is not punishing us for this perversion of justice, we are simply living in the fruit of this mentality. Our "punishment" is the fruit of our doings. God did not want us to live in the results of this kind of mentality, that's why He warned us, yet we chose to reject His wisdom and depend on our own. This gives us an opportunity to be in control. We can get our needs met without trusting God and His wisdom.

Remember, control is the bottom line for the codependent. What greater way to control you than to make you dependent on me. So my political party offers to meet this need for you and that need

for you and, ultimately, you will need me. You will
not trust God. You will not even trust yourself.
You will trust me. You will vote for me and give me
your loyalty because I will meet your needs.

Our nation is suffering from a self-worth
crisis. In this environment of low self-worth, people
are looking to someone to meet their needs and give
them security. In exchange, they will surrender
their freedom, their dignity, and their confidence in
God.

16

THE POWER OF PARENTING

There is little in this life that will affect us as much as the influence of our parents. Some experts say our basic beliefs about life and ourselves are established before we are five years old. Before we are old enough to reason it all out, someone else has determined the way we will see the world. Because of a departure from godly, Bible-based principles of child-raising and a gravitation toward negative religious concepts, many well-meaning parents have rooted their children in a dysfunctional lifestyle that leads to codependency. Between the misunderstanding of Biblical principles and the humanistic philosophies of the world, the average parent has been hard pressed to find the answers to raise emotionally healthy children.

The extremely negative, dominating concepts of child-raising presented by the religious legalist don't appeal to loving, gentle parents. They want to do what the Word of God says, but the punitive approach just doesn't "sit right." These extreme interpretations of the Word of God force people to look to other sources to find principles for child-raising. The humanistic approach was gentler and more loving, yet it still left children just as dysfunctional as the legalistic, religious approach. This, however, has been the choice of many

Christians.

Because so many parents felt they were unqualified to read, understand, and apply the Bible, they failed to find the simple solutions offered in the Word. They failed to understand that *agape* love has to be the guiding factor in all relationships, including the relationships with our children. According to 1 Corinthians 13:8, *"Love never ceases to be effective."* AMP

When we don't know what else will work, we should always know that love will work. This is what God does for us, He keeps on loving us. He keeps on being good to us and the *". . .goodness of God leads us to repentance."* Romans 2:4. Most people are afraid of walking in love. Because of a liberal, unscriptural concept of love, they are afraid that walking in love will make them vulnerable.

Love, however, is the only way to *keep* from being taken advantage of. If I accept God's definition of love, I will not accept yours, therefore, you cannot control me with guilt. You can ask me to love you, but only God can define how that love is to operate. Although I love you, I will probably not do everything that you want. Jesus didn't do everything people wanted. He was not a push over. No one took advantage of Him, yet all that He did, He did in love. He got tough. He drove the money changers out of the temple with a whip. He confronted the Pharisees and the religious leaders about their destruction of God's people.

All the actions Jesus took were motivated by His love for God and His love for people. He was never motivated by anger. The Bible says, *"Be ye angry, and sin not: let not the sun go down upon your wrath."* Ephesians 4:26. Our problem is, we don't realize we can be angry and resist sin at the same time. When we walk in love, all that we do is for the benefit of the person we are dealing with. All that we do has its basis in the Word of God. The moment we surrender one of these two guiding posts, we are no longer walking in love. Ask yourself, "Am I doing this for the benefit of the person? Is this consistent with the Word of God?"

Many well-meaning parents have done the things they did for the good of their child, but their interpretation of the Word of God caused it to be ineffective. As Christians, we tend to become like the God we believe in. If we believe God is quick to punish, we will be quick to punish. If we believe God is long suffering, we will be long suffering. If we think God is angry at those who sin, we will be angry at those who sin.

Because we have accepted the concept of an angry God, we have become angry Christians. We are quick to judge and slow to forgive. We are anxious to discover and reveal the faults of others. Where this does the most damage is with our children. We fill them with rejection and insecurity. They are often unsure of our love or God's love. Because of the God we depict, our children are anxious to leave the church and leave our beliefs.

Our concept of Christianity places the highest emphasis on being right, so we try to make our kids do right. In this process, worth starts being determined by how right one is. If one is not right, then they have no value. In our attempt to make our children do right, we often dominate, control, reject, or overprotect. Thus, the dysfunction begins.

As parents, our first priority should be to make our children feel loved. I am not talking about spoiling them or giving in to their every whim, but we should make it our goal to cause our children to experience our love. If children do not become confident in the love of the parents, they will seldom become confident in the love of God.

As parents, we must realize that our children belong to God, not to us. We are not preparing them to please us in life; we are preparing them to have a relationship with the Lord and please Him. We "cast the die" concerning our children's ability to relate to the Lord. They tend to transfer the experiences with their parents onto their concepts of God.

We are not raising them to be successful in business as much as we are raising them to be successful in life and relationships. Our children need the relationship skills that come very naturally from a strong sense of love and self-worth. The ability to have meaningful relationships is the most important skill we can ever pass on to our children. It will determine their happiness more than any other single factor. How much money they make will not effect their happiness as much as their ability to relate to others.

When children do not feel a sense of love and worth from their parents, they will develop the need to look to others to meet this need. They will not be capable of objective, healthy friendships. They will become codependent takers. When they are confident in our love, however, it will be an easy thing to convince them of the love God has for them. They will ultimately turn to the one unfailing source of love and worth, God the Father. They will relate to their Heavenly Father much like they have related to us and they will relate to others in a positive, healthy way.

Without realizing it, we can put our children into a "works-righteousness mentality" if we withhold love from them when they displease us and reward them with affection when they do please us. After a while, they will develop an association that says love and acceptance is earned. Then in their relationship with God, they never feel like sons, they always feel like hired help. They feel they must be right to earn God's love.

We have failed to develop the ability to express displeasure without expressing rejection. We have failed to understand how to withhold privileges without withholding affection. We don't know how to be angry and sin not. We don't know how to say no and still portray love.

The overprotecting and controlling parent creates just as much dysfunction as the abusive parent, sometimes more. The abused child is exposed to open, obvious rejection. Because it is overt, they understand why they struggle with self-worth. It is sometimes easier for them to accept their parents dysfunction and disassociate themselves from their parents problems.

A controlling, overprotective parent, however, conveys a total lack of confidence to the child. Because the parent makes all of the decisions ,the child assumes that he is too dumb to make decisions. This can be done in such a subtle way that the child cannot identify the dysfunction of the parent. They cannot see that the parent is a codependent controller. They do not understand their feelings of inadequacy or their anger at their parent.

The child of a controller lacks confidence to such a degree that he feels guilty for even questioning his parent. The parent has proven them wrong at nearly every decision. How could it be my parent? He is always right. This child is much less likely to ever be free than the child who was abused or openly rejected.

One of the things that most children are cheated out of is the opportunity to experience failure and still feel good about themselves. So much emphasis is placed on the need to be right, that the child feels shame and disgrace when he fails. This can easily bring about all sorts of extreme reactions and can position the child to spend a lifetime trying to prove himself right. He is set to be a codependent controller who needs for people to think he is right.

The two main goals of parenting should be making our children feel loved and teaching them responsibility. These two will balance one another. Responsibility without love can be hard and mean. Love without responsibility can be liberal and undermining. But, love and responsibility will bring a child to maturity without the loss of self-worth.

Most of the church's ministry to children is attempting to reach the children the last generation of Christians lost. Then after we reach them, we spend a lifetime trying to heal them from the hurts that the last generation of confused Christian parents inflicted upon them.

An elderly man in Canada, after all of his children were grown stated, "I think child-raising should be 90% affirmation and 10% confrontation." I think he's right. If we, as parents, can affirm our love for our children and build a healthy self-worth through our love and the love of God, I think they will be able to face and win the game of life. If children are not dealing with the issues of self-worth and rejection, they will be free to place their attention on the task at hand.

A child with a healthy self-worth is not subject to peer pressure. He doesn't need the acceptance of the group to such a degree that he falls into the traps of adolescence. Because we have missed the objectives of parenting, our children spend their adult years trying to find what is easiest found as a child; self-worth!

17

MENTAL HEALTH

Mental health is such a broad topic. It is not developed from one source. It is more of a combination of influences that come together to create our life paradigms. Every bit of information we are exposed to and every experience we ever have is a part of producing our state of mental health. However, this country has been lulled into a false hope of mental health that feeds the codependent mindset.

There seems to be at least two streams of conflicting thought among those who search for ways to establish emotional stability in man. There are those who see man's need to accept responsibility for his actions. These professionals are very close to the Biblical approach to mental health. Then there is another stream of thought that focuses on finding the cause of emotional instability. This group seems to be more concerned with placing blame than placing responsibility.

In the mental health field, it seems there is a belief that says, "If you can find someone to blame then you don't have to feel guilty about your problems. If you don't feel guilty about your problems, you will get better." That has more reality than some would like to admit. After a person is freed from guilt, they must still assume responsibility. Knowing who to blame has never set anyone free.

Some of the greatest breakthroughs in mental health have occurred in the past twenty years. Some researchers are finally realizing that the mechanical model of man was totally incorrect. In some areas of behavioral psychology, people are moving closer to a Biblical concept of man. Although most people in these fields or in the church, don't realize how close they are coming to the Biblical model in some areas.

Society has been duped by the mental health *"experts"* in the past. Stop and think of it. We have people who only believe in the physical world specializing in the area of thoughts. This is the very realm of existence they deny, the non-physical. If that is not breeding ground for contradiction, I don't know what is.

Since we cannot see the spirit or soul of a man and we can only observe the reactions, no one can measure thought, worry, fear, happiness, peace, love or any other emotion. All we can do is measure some of the body's responses to those emotions. Therefore, there is always a certain amount of speculation about any conclusions concerning emotions.

This dilemma makes it easy for researchers to begin their research with all sorts of unproven theories. These theories determine in advance how we will interpret all of our data. Thus, our research is tainted from the beginning. Every experiment must begin with certain absolutes, therefore, those who study the mind begin with some concepts that they consider to be absolute. But what if their predetermined concepts are wrong? The way they interpret all of their data will be wrong.

The liberal believes that religion is the cause

of man's problems. He has had religious values imposed upon him, therefore, he has a false sense of guilt about his actions. He falsely asserts that if he had no religious beliefs or moral standards, he would have no sense of guilt. After all, he surmises, there is no right or wrong. The liberal's cure for man is to cast off all restraints and fulfill his every passion.[1] Society has sought this path of recovery only to find themselves sinking deeper into the trap of instability and codependency.

When I first read the Bible, I remember coming to this phrase, *"The soul that sinneth shall die."* Ezekiel 18:4, 20. When I asked my pastor what the Bible meant when it talked about a soul, he said, "Soul is just another word for person." It made sense, the Bible speaks of 3000 souls being saved. It seemed like it was talking about people. Yet, as I looked at the various passages that mentioned the soul, I realized it was more than a synonym for a person. It was speaking of a specific part of a person. It was talking about the mind and emotions.

Then I began to see that sin destroys the soul, i.e. the mind and emotions. People did not fall over dead when they committed a particular sin, but they did experience a degree of death in their soul. Proverbs 8:36 says, *"He that sinneth against me wrongeth his own soul."* When we violate the wisdom of God, there are negative effects in the soul.

The destruction that works in our soul is not the work of an angry, vengeful God. It is like trying to make your engine run on water. It is destructive. It doesn't work. Many times, I have heard people say, "If only we had gotten an operator's manual for life. . ." Well, we did. We just don't like what it says. God created us. He knows what will bring us life and what will bring us death. He gave us the information we need. We simply don't trust Him.

The world says it is the lack of fulfilling your desire that is destroying you. Go for it! Do what you want. Then you'll be happy. Wrong! Then you'll be emotionally unstable. Proverbs 6:32 says, *"But whoso committeth adultery with a woman lacketh understanding: he that doeth it destroyeth his own soul."* The world says, "If you want her, that's the only way you'll ever be fulfilled."

The world has led us running down the path to destruction. A loving God is saying, "Please don't do those things. They will kill you." But we have stopped our ears and said, "I don't trust you. You don't want me to be happy. That's why you won't let me sin."

We have this concept that sin is the list of fun things God will not let us do. It is as if He made all of the fun things sin so He could somehow test us. Wrong! Sin is a list of all those things that will kill you. Sin will rob you of emotional health.

The church has failed miserably at presenting the issue of sin to the world. We have made it a matter of right and wrong, good and bad. This will never be enough motivation for a person to leave sin. Once the world believes that sin will cause them pain, they will leave it alone. Once they see that godliness will produce joy, they will want it. We have simply not presented it to them in a wise manner.

The second basic flaw of our mental health system is its desire to find someone to blame. This is food for the codependent mind. There is a difference between peace and relief. Peace comes from God. Relief can come from many sources. I used to get relief by doing drugs. I would get relief by committing adultery. I got relief from a lot of destructive sources. Finding someone to blame gives relief, not peace. But relief never lasts.

Why do people spend a lifetime in therapy? Simple, they need to keep getting temporary doses of relief. When people experience the peace of God, they don't need relief anymore. They don't need someone to blame. It doesn't matter who caused the problem.

I am constantly amazed at the rational of some counselors. A dysfunctional person will sit in a counseling session and give their version of their problems to their counselor and he doesn't even check to see if they're true or accurate. Instead, he gathers all the information about who did what to the poor victim, calls for the family members to come in, and then they are all made to feel responsible for the patient's problems.

I have seen parents of problem children assassinated by mental health counselors. It was as if the entire family was crazy and this person, who is now in the mental ward, is the only sane one in the group. What's wrong with this picture?

A counselor never knows if their patient is truthful or not. Many emotionally unstable people are very effective liars. They have spent a lifetime making the irrational and untrue seem rational and true. The one and only thing a counselor can deal with is whether or not their patient is responding to the people around him in a responsible way.

Sadly, these "professionals" have now become the heart and soul of the criminal justice system. They have taken their bizarre form of interpretation into our courtrooms and made the criminal to be the victim. His past somehow frees him from the consequences of his actions.

The criminal justice system does not exist to rehabilitate the criminal. I think there should be tremendous attempts made to rehabilitate criminals, but not in the court room. The justice system is there to protect the rights of the innocent. Criminals are not put in jail to punish them as much as they are put in jail to protect society. Rehabilitation is another issue altogether.

Our mental health system in this country has invaded the classroom, the court room and the living room. People who operate from unproven theories are controlling the way we perceive the treatment and prevention of the emotionally unstable, yet, their very philosophies ensure that mental disorders will grow out of control. Codependency will be nurtured and society will be crippled.

Our approach to mental health has failed miserably. Some research has shown that the same percentage of people will improve whether they do or do not receive treatment from a mental health expert.[2] Which means our system is not working.

By rejecting God's method of mental health, which the church has poorly represented, we have given ourselves over to those whose own methods have failed. . . the experts.

---

[1] *The Christian Counselor's Manual,* Jay Adams, Baker Book House, Grand Rapids, Michigan

[2] Ibid.

18

EDUCATION

America once had the greatest education system in the world, but today we are falling behind other nations in the quality of education we provide for our children. The problem with education, however, is not because we do not have the right information to teach our children. It is because of the beliefs and agendas of those who control the education system.

It was not enough that the educators removed the mention of God from the class room, they removed all principles of development and tutoring that were consistent with Biblical principles of training children. Everything that the Bible teaches that will make one responsible, stable and have good self-worth, has been replaced by mere theories that are not working and never will work.

The effort to return prayer to the classroom is valiant and I agree with it, but it will not come close to dealing with the real problem. What we need is godly teachers in the classroom, on the board of education, on the city council, in the court rooms and in the White House. There are no simple solutions. Prayer, without a return to Biblical principles, will never make a noticeable difference.

Children cannot build a sense of self-worth if they cannot identify with God as their Creator. For a child to think that he is the offspring of some amoeba that swam up out of a swamp is not the breeding ground for good self-worth, nor for the respect of human life, in general.

If children are not made to be responsible for their actions, they cannot be taught. The courts have disempowered teachers by taking away authority and giving more responsibility. The concept of education as a right instead of a privilege, has taken all power away from the teacher and the educational process. Education, however, is a privilege that belongs to parents and children who will yield themselves to the process.

Several years ago, I visited a first grade classroom in our city to discuss some education problems with my daughter. The teacher openly confessed, "I don't have time to teach, I simply try to keep the class under control." The hands of the teacher have been tied by the legal issues, the political system, and the special interest groups. These groups have no value for the child or education, they simply have an interest in having things their way.

Only the successful have earned the right to teach. The Bible says, *"That ye be not slothful, but followers of them who through faith and patience inherit the promises."* Hebrews 6:12. We should only follow those who have succeeded by observing Biblical principles, yet, we have people with no success in life dictating how the education process should work. We have those whose children are in trouble telling us how their children should be handled. Textbooks are written by rebellious "rejects" with an agenda. This doesn't just happen at the primary level, it continues all the way through college.

I once needed some people to work in a

business I owned. I knew part-time people could do the job, so I went to one of the local universities. I met with the head of the business department to discuss my desire to hire students. I felt it would be good for the students to give them an opportunity at real business while they were still in school.

The more I talked with this man, the more frustrated I became. As he described his philosophies of business, I determined I didn't want to hire anyone that had his mentality. As I talked further with him, I found that he had never started or managed a business. In fact, he had never had a job other than teaching. He didn't have a clue about the real world.

Think of it, the government that regulates the laws for business does not create one dollar of profit for the country. Many of the people in political offices never had a real job. They are professional politicians. They have wrecked our economy, yet, they tell us how to run our businesses and educate our children. I think this qualifies for "the blind leading the blind."

Our educational system spends twelve years steeping our children in living out of control, proving that there are no serious consequences for actions, clearly establishing that one can get by with little or no effort, and all the while providing one of the most inferior education's of all the industrialized world. The facts bear this out; our education system has failed. To add insult to injury, there are laws that require us to have our children educated by these failures and, in some states, we can't even choose our school of choice.

Much of the material that is taught in school is inaccurate. It has been rewritten to leave out any mention of God or godliness. It has made our heroes into villains and has undermined our confidence in our country, our values and our God. To read some text books would lead you to believe that communism worked. It seems that the goal of education has little to do with teaching children academically and much more to do with forming their opinions and values.

There is a subtle and even sometimes overt message sent forth to the students that their parents are not the final authority. The child is made to believe that the state is the ultimate parent. All of the devaluating of the family becomes another important factor in undermining identity and self-worth, all of which creates a deep need to find a source of identity and worth. The humanistic educator is more than glad to facilitate this need. It may actually be his goal.

Remember, however, this is not a diabolical conspiracy. This is just the world system. This is man depending on himself and others for that which he should only depend on God. These are people who truly want to make the world a better place to live and raise children. These are the children of parents who departed from God. The world leaders of today are the codependent children of yesterday's faithless society.

As far as these people have drifted from God, that still does not mean they are a deliberate, willing part of a sinister plot. The more the church attacks them, the farther they withdraw from God and His wisdom. We need to demonstrate the effects of godliness. They need to see our godliness affect our cities and schools. They need to see us have peace and success within the body of Christ.

The farther the educators move from God, the farther they move from an understanding of His entire creation. Planet earth has become a trash heap of toxic waste. Governments are corrupt. People are needlessly starving. Disease is running out of control. All of this is the product of people departing from God's wisdom.

God created man and placed him in an environment that is conducive to his needs. The first rebellion in the garden brought about the first environmental changes in planet earth. It brought the introduction of pain, sickness and suffering. As man has lost touch with God, he has lost touch with his need to function in a healthy, social and physical environment. This loss of the big picture has given rise to the era of the specialists.

Specialists focus on one part to such an extent that they lose touch with the whole. The specialist makes phenomenal inventions, but the by-product of those inventions create toxic waste. The medical specialist gives a medication that kills one sickness while causing five others. The economic specialists keep the economy strong while creating financial disaster for the small businessman. The human rights specialists help the poor at the cost of the middle class. The religious specialist gets people to heaven, but doesn't have a clue about how to live effectively in this life. The education specialist can teach a particular subject with no understanding of the values that must undergird that learning process.

In 1979, a group of academic specialists admitted to the Washington Post that they did not know how to solve global problems. We have had so many years of focusing in on the individual details that we have lost the whole picture. When people do not understand God's plan for man, they desperately grasp for the meaning of life. Everyone

desperately hopes that their little bit of knowledge
will be the key that changes it all. Desperation,
greed and ignorance lead us to a specialized,
idealistic society. We offer people false hope if they
will just trust our plan or our idea. The truth is,
there is no freedom for the saint nor the sinner
apart from knowing and trusting God.

There is a battle waging for the minds of our
children. So far, the church has lost. We have
inexperienced, codependent controllers forming the
paradigms of the youth. In the name of education,
they are being led down the primrose path of
codependency. Like the youth of Nazi Germany or
the young communists, they are being offered a
utopia that only exists in the minds of emotionally
unstable people. Their lives and ideas are being
forged by the idealistic, codependent controller.

19

CHRISTIAN MENTAL HEALTH

Because man has not trusted God, he has looked to every other source in the world to find the answers to emotional health. But the more theories man comes up with, the more mental and emotional sicknesses that sweep down on our society. Year by year, as we have cast away God's standards, we dove deeper and deeper into a crisis that is giving rise to every imaginable horror. The arrogant unbeliever insists that if we will just reject more of God's standards, we will ultimately find the manmade utopia.

Since there is not a single scientist that can explain the processes of the brain, much less the mind, I feel that I should reconsider who I take my advice from. The only theories of man that have worked are the ones that have been consistent with the Word of God. Therefore, I must look to the Word of God for absolute information about the mind and emotions.

We must be careful to separate the teaching of the church and the teaching of the Bible. Unfortunately, many theories of the church are as inconsistent with the Word of God as the theories of the world. It has been these unscriptural, unworkable concepts of the church, that have caused serious-minded people to look to another source for authoritative answers.

In Genesis, God created man's body from the dust of the earth. He then breathed into man something of Himself, some of His own Spirit. When these two elements came together, man did not become a living **body**, as the medical world would have us to believe. Nor did he become a living **spirit**, as the religious world would have us to believe. God's Word says that man became a living **soul**! *"And the LORD God formed man of the dust of the ground, and breathed into his nostrils the breath of life; and man became a living soul."* Genesis 2:7.

Man's body is what keeps him alive to this world. He can feel things in the physical world. Those physical feelings are turned into thoughts and emotions in the soul. Likewise, the spirit of a man gives him awareness of the spiritual world. That information also becomes feelings and emotions in the soul. Man experiences and interprets both spiritual and physical life in the realm of the soul.

Since God created man, He is the only one who really fully understands how real mental health should work. Everything we need to know about mental health should be found in the Bible and supported by scientific experimentation—if either of these two groups could give up their prejudices and work together. But, regardless of scientific validation, time has proven that the principles of the Word of God work consistently.

"And this is life eternal, that they might know thee the only true God, and Jesus Christ, whom thou hast sent." John 17:3. When the Bible talks about life, it talks about a particular quality of life. The Greek word is *zoe*. *Zoe* life is the quality of life as possessed by the one who gives it.[1] In this case, we

are speaking of the quality of life God has. This is what Jesus came to give.

Jesus said this quality of life would be the product of knowing God. Knowing God is the product of a relationship, not just a singular experience. While it is absolutely essential that we have a "born again" experience, that experience alone will not produce *zoe*. If we don't develop a relationship with God and find fullness of life, that experience can be frustrating and cause us to disbelieve.

In the Old Testament, there were people who believed in God, but they never had the opportunity to experience this quality of life. This can only be found in the finished work of Jesus. By accepting the love of God as expressed through the Lord Jesus' finished work, we can be brought into a realm where we experience *zoe*.

Through Jesus, we have complete peace with God. *"Therefore being justified by faith, we have peace with God through our Lord Jesus Christ."* Romans 5:1. True mental health is only found when man is at peace with God in his own heart. That peace only comes when one trusts the reality that Jesus has not only died to become their Savior, He has also risen again to become their righteousness.

This meets the deepest need that man has. This is the basis for all emotional health. This is the stabilizing factor that brings all of life together. But this is also the reality that the church and the world have rejected. Both groups have rejected the truth, neither one realizing the implications. Both groups have robbed man of the one and only thing that would bring him absolute stability and peace, the qualification for the total love and acceptance of

God.

Romans, chapter 9, talks about Jesus being the stumbling stone. But, it really doesn't talk about Him **personally** being the stumbling stone. It talks about the faith righteousness which is found in Jesus being the stumbling stone. *"What shall we say then? That the Gentiles, which followed not after righteousness, have attained to righteousness, even the righteousness which is of faith. But Israel, which followed after the law of righteousness, hath not attained to the law of righteousness Wherefore? Because they sought it not by faith, but as it were by the works of the law. For they stumbled at that stumblingstone; As it is written, Behold, I lay in Sion a stumblingstone and rock of offense: and whosoever believeth on him shall not be ashamed."* Romans 9:30-33.

The Gentiles were not looking for righteousness, but, they found it. Why? They were willing to accept it as a free gift. Israel, on the other hand, was trying desperately to find righteousness so they could be accepted by God. They could not find it. Why? They refused to believe it could be received as a free gift. They stumbled at the stumbling stone. Jesus as Savior is not the stumbling stone, Jesus as our righteousness is the stumbling stone.

Faith righteousness is the best kept secret in the church. Preachers preach day and night trying to get people to work harder to be more righteous so they can be accepted of God. It is this load that the Jews could not carry, and neither can we. This is why Jesus came. We didn't just need a way to get to heaven, we needed freedom from the guilt of sin and the burden of righteousness. By making us righteous, we now have complete peace with God.

It is this burden of responsibility that has made the world turn its back on God. The world was smart enough to know that no one could ever be righteous enough to please a perfect God. Laboring under that load has driven many people completely crazy. So the world said, "Nobody can do this, so why try? Let's erase the mention of God from our memory so we can be free from trying to please Him. Then maybe we can get on with life." The church and the world have both stumbled over the stumbling stone: Jesus Christ, our righteousness.

The human mind can only function optimally when it is at peace. The absence of peace is destructive to both body and soul. Peace is only found in a meaningful, loving relationship with God through the Lord Jesus. It is found in a place where we accept the finished work of Jesus. We have received Him as Lord, Savior and **righteousness.** Nothing else brings absolute peace.

Many Christians have lost emotional stability believing that Jesus was Lord, but not knowing if God would accept them. Trying to qualify is the torment of the Christian. Trying to qualify destroys self-worth. Trying to qualify makes a statement to the heart that says, "I am not qualified." This is the cause of condemnation, the Christian insanity.

Condemnation is the expectation of judgment.[2]   If one is not fully convinced that Jesus met all of our qualifications for righteousness, he will only have one other source of comfort and peace: his performance. This means one must become a totally deceived, self-righteous legalist or ride the roller coaster of performance. When we perform well, we are self-righteous; when we do not perform well, we feel guilty. Guilt has to do with punishment. When one feels guilty, they expect things to go wrong. It is this fear that becomes the breeding ground for physical and emotional instability.

Neither the totally false concepts of the world, nor the warped religious concepts of the church have been able to provide man with the peace and stability offered in the Word of God. Both systems are failing and neither one wants to admit it. The world may ignore God, but the need that every man has to know and feel the love of God will not go away. The incidence of addiction, immorality, violence, insanity and other social ills will continue to grow as the world moves farther from the God that loves them.

The religious church will continue to be an impotent force in the world. It will hold out promises that are not fulfilled in this life. It will only experience small degrees of victory. Fortunately, the church may fail a man in this life, but it will not fail in eternity. The world system may bring some relief in this life, but it will fail in eternity.

Either of these extremes, however, will prevent a man from knowing God and finding *zoe'* a quality of emotional and physical life that can only be found in God.

[1] *Biblico-Theological Lexicon of New Testament Greek,* Hermann Cremer, Edinburgh: T & T Clark, 38 George Street

[2] T*hayer's Greek-English Lexicon of the New Testament,* Baker Book House, Grand Rapids, MI

SECTION 3:

THE

CODEPENDENT

CHURCH

SECTION 3:
INTRODUCTION

Let me begin this section by saying I love the church. With all its flaws and failures, the church is my family. It is not my desire to cast stones, nor is it my intention to undermine your confidence in the church. Yet, it is essential that the church examine itself to see if it is *"in the faith."*

The church went into the dark ages by departing from the teaching of the Lord Jesus. The reformation did not bring us out of the dark ages, it simply turned on a few lights. Many of the very beliefs that took the church into darkness still abound in a milder form. It is essential that we recognize and understand what is at work in the church, so that we can avoid its pitfalls.

The early church organized around carnal concepts of carnal men. Christianity became the excuse for greedy, power-hungry men to conquer the world. They probably always wanted to conquer the world, only now they had a just cause to justify their quest for power. The agenda for organization was not one of godliness, it was one of power and control. To this day, one of the great struggles within the church is control.

I truly believe that many of the leaders that disempower God's people, do it with the greatest of intentions. I do not believe the problem is wicked, evil leaders as much as it is ignorant, unbelieving leaders. Every leader is, to some degree, the product of what he has been taught. He is simply continuing in what has been passed down from generation to generation with little thought about the effects.

In my years of preaching grace, peace, the love of God, dignity and worth and other empowering realities, I have only had extreme, negative reactions from those who feared losing control of the people. There is so little trust for God, that pastors don't even trust God to take care of His own children. We have become like the teenage baby sitter who thinks she knows more than the parents.

Leaders are afraid that if we lose control of the people, they will run wildly into sin. Yet, we never face the reality that they are already struggling with sin. Our attempts may have been noble and valiant, but they still are not really working. We have fallen into the codependent world system. We trust our vain attempts at control that have failed, more than we trust God.

This section will challenge all of us. It will make us question everything that we have trusted, other than God, Himself. It will call for us to bring things into perspective. It will remove the blinders that have kept us from the life and power of God. For some, it may be the first time since your conversion that you will once again have the opportunity to truly trust God.

My greatest concern in writing this section is what the codependent thinker will twist this into. The codependent is great at placing blame. Some may use this as an opportunity to blame the church or some pastor for their failures. If this is your temptation, let that be the greatest proof that this is talking about you. No one in the church has ever used you or taken advantage of you without your cooperation.[1]

There is also the person who will feel the spotlight is on him. Because the opportunity to assume responsibility and bring about change seems like placing blame, you may respond in anger. Please accept this as a codependent tendency that will keep you trapped where you are. I am not interested in placing blame. I am, however, interested in exposing the workings of codependency, so that we can escape the subtle trap that has been laid for us.

The church can only be a powerful, positive force in the world when the people that make up the church are whole. The church can continue in its codependent quest for control and false security, or it can set people free to experience God. When the church leaves the codependent principles upon which it has operated, it will experience true revival within and real evangelism without.

---

[1] *My Church My Family: How to Have a Healthy Relationship with the Church*, Dr. James B. Richards, Impact Ministries, Huntsville, Alabama

20

SWAPPING ADDICTIONS

It is nearly impossible to escape the codependent trap in our society. People's ability to have meaningful relationships is at an all time low. Divorce, child abuse, violent crime and the tremendous increase in substance abuse all attest the fact that social problems are getting worse, not better. All of this is the product of a faithless society that has created monumental emotional needs in its people.

I have heard it said, "Codependency is the mother of all addictions," and it does give rise to every kind of addiction and abuse. At the heart of every substance abuse problem you will find a socially inept person. The absence of experiencing the love of God leaves a person desperately in need. It is like having a thirst that can't be quenched; that's why the alcoholic drinks. It's like having a longing unfulfilled; that's why the drug addict craves. It's like an inescapable loneliness; that's why the sex addict lusts. It's a great emptiness we try to fill with everything imaginable, but none of these substitutes ever meet the need.

Then we hear about Jesus. We see something in the life of a Christian; we hear hope in the sermon of a preacher; we hear life in the words of a believer and we allow ourselves to hope one more time. Something about all of it rings true. We know inside that this is what we have longed for. So, we surrender our life to Jesus.

Far too many times, however, instead of entering a meaningful relationship with God, we simply exchange one codependent lifestyle for another. Most people are never set free from their addictions; they simply exchange them for a new type of addiction that is more socially acceptable. It may not be as socially destructive, but it is still an addiction. Once again we accept the offer of false security in exchange for a living relationship.

Often, the codependent will go into a good church that is not trying to create codependency, but because of his own desires, he creates a codependent situation. He forms an unhealthy dependency on the pastor, counselors or a particular person. Going to church, talking the talk, and playing the game becomes his new way to find approval. He is often doing all the right things for all the wrong reasons and he is once again left empty.

Unfortunately, many churches unknowingly play into the game of the codependent. In fact, many churches unknowingly and unintentionally are set up to reward and nurture codependency.

The church has become so ingrained with the philosophies of the world system that the codependent comes in, unconsciously identifies the system and immediately continues in the same routine that he worked in the world. All he has to do is change his terminology and he's in. We don't say, "I will earn your approval." We say, "I'm committed brother." We no longer call it bondage, now we call it submitted. We no longer say, "I want to run your life." Now it's, "I have a word from the Lord." Same system, different lingo.

I was recently ministering to someone from China. She had not been in America very long. She was horrified at what she found in the American church. She said, "This is just like communism. We had meetings that you were obligated to attend. We sang songs that motivated us. The speaker had a little book that he spoke from. You were to follow the leader without question. If you questioned the leader, you were considered a trouble maker. The American church is just like communism."

It is not the mere similarity of how the two groups functioned that was so unnerving for this and other former communists to whom I have ministered, it is the similarity in attitude. It is the similarity in the way the system works. There are the same dogmas, the same controls, and the same quests for power.

For over twenty years, I have seen people come to Jesus only to become totally disillusioned by the carnality of the church. These people realized that it was not much different in the church than it was in the world. No doubt this is not always the church's fault; but by and large, the church is set up to thrive on codependency, just like the world system.

Without a doubt, a religious person has more potential to be mean and hard than almost any other kind of person. Religion has started and sustained wars. People are murdered every day somewhere in the world based on religious beliefs. Religion is not the same as Christianity. Religion is the world's system, Christianity is God's system. Religion is man's attempt to reach God on his own terms. Christianity is the terms that God has presented to man. Religion is man-centered. Christianity is God-centered. Religion works from the basis of disempowerment and control. Christianity works from the basis of empowerment and responsibility.

One of the biggest differences between religion and Christianity is faith. Faith is trust for God and His integrity. Faith produces a healthy dependency on God. A healthy dependence on God stimulates a healthy inter-dependence on others. Religion is codependent. It is built around a lack of trust for God and His terms. Therefore, it produces a fear of God that discourages a healthy relationship. It encourages dependence on man and ceremonies to provide the securities that should come from God.

Before a person can become a mean, angry, and religious legalist, they must first be codependent. Religion has nothing to do with trusting God. It has to do with finding security apart from God. It has to do with controlling people and circumstances to meet the needs in their life that should be met through God.

For the codependent, religion is a natural, comfortable move from one addiction to another. He accepts forgiveness of sins, but never enters into a meaningful relationship with God. He is on his way to heaven, yet dysfunctional in this life. He is susceptible to all the religious extremes that offer security. He chases every man, tries every formula, feels victimized and in the end blames God. *"The foolishness of man perverteth his way: and his heart fretteth against the LORD."* Proverbs 19:3.

Religious codependency can be as destructive in this life as any other addiction. The religious addict can become an extremist who alienates his children because of his idealistic expectations. It can be the wife who drives her husband away because he is not spiritual enough. It can be the person who goes into depression because he feels he can never live up to what he believes to be God's standards. It can be the David Koresh or Jim Jones who justifies murder for religious reasons. It can be the man or woman who neglects their family in an attempt to be committed to the local church.

Religious codependency, however, has the power to do something that no other addiction can do. It has the power to turn people away from God. It has the power to cause people to run from the gospel. It makes people ashamed of the church. It can cost people their eternal salvation. It presents an image of God to the world that is unattractive and undesirable.

For the codependent, it assures that he will never experience freedom. He will never have intimacy with God. He will spend his life attempting to find security in his doctrines, his ceremonies, and the approval of other men.

The codependent places his confidence and security in the most deadly religious addictions, legalism or ritualism. If he doesn't find his security in these, he would have to find it in a real relationship with God. A relationship is the most threatening of all things to the codependent. It is what he wants more than anything, but what he will never let himself experience. His self-centered attempts to protect himself and get his needs met, will keep him from freedom. He merely gives up his worldly addiction for some religious addictions.

21

WORLDLY SUCCESS

One of the first things that must happen in the life of any believer is to renew his mind. It will be your mind that gets you into trouble. It is the mind (soul) where every battle will rage. (1 Peter 2:11) It will be the way that you think that will keep the power of God from working in your life. (Romans 8:7) It will be the way you think that leads you into life's struggles.

If you still think the way you previously thought, you will simply "Christianize" your methods and terminology, and plod ahead with the same methods you used in the world. This has been the plight of the church for eighteen hundred years. We have struggled with the simple truths of serving, yielding, trusting, and surrendering as taught by the Lord Jesus. We could not see how these things would lead us into victory. Because we could not reason these things out, we rejected them. We depended on our wisdom and rejected the wisdom of God.

After all, we have spent a lifetime working a particular system. Why change now? Now that we're straight and sober, we can work this system. We erroneously think the only thing wrong with the old system was me. Now that I'm not a mess, the old plan I had should work. We fail to realize it wasn't just us that was a mess before Jesus, it was also the plan we were working.

We have spent a lifetime working the world's system. It's the only system we know. But, now we are *"in the world but not of the world."* We are aliens on planet earth. We have our citizenship in heaven. We are citizens of the Kingdom of God. We must learn to live in that "system." We must learn the principles that operate in the Kingdom of God. Principles like giving of self, serving, trusting God, walking in love, and placing others before ourselves.

We should have received a warning sticker when we got saved that said, "WARNING THE TRUTH ONLY WORKS IN THE KINGDOM OF GOD!" It's like buying the best appliance in the world, but having an electrical current that is incompatible. It just doesn't work. This does not mean that the principles of God do not work in this life, it simply means they only work when motivated by love, based on the Word, and dependent on grace.

The church desires to succeed and we should. We have a call to succeed. We are to *"occupy (do business and gain ground) until He returns."*[1] We should be winning the world. We should be making disciples unto the Lord Jesus. We should be the thriving force in the world. But we should not abandon the faith to accomplish these goals. We should know how to empty ourselves and walk in God's power. But we don't.

We use the right words, but when it comes down to it, we're just working our plan in our strength and asking God to bless it. We don't know His plan, nor how to walk in His strength. This is foreign to the unrenewed mind. We are trying to do all we can **for** God, instead of doing all we can **with**

God. We are willing to praise Him for what happens in our strength because we don't really trust His strength.

The Promise Bible says, *"From the time of John the Baptist until now violent people have been trying to take over the Kingdom of Heaven by force."* Matthew 11:12. The church rejected Jesus' teaching and has tried to take the Kingdom of God by force. We have turned everything into a carnal attempt to do the things of God. It's not that the church is not trying to fulfill the commission of Jesus, the problem is, we are using the world's methods and principles.

We are like the sons of thunder who wanted to call down fire on the cities that rejected their message. *"And when his disciples James and John saw this, they said, Lord, wilt thou that we command fire to come down from heaven, and consume them, even as Elias did? But he turned, and rebuked them, and said, Ye know not what manner of spirit ye are of."* Luke 9:54-55.

These disciples wanted to use force to turn people to Jesus. They were willing to abandon all the attributes of love to get the success they wanted. I guess they thought the end would justify the means. This is too much like the church today. We will accomplish the task if we have to stay in the flesh everyday to do it. So the church turns to the same tactics as the world. There is no difference, only the terminology has been changed to disguise the truth.

Before Jesus left planet earth, the disciples were arguing over who would be in charge. They were already planning how they would rule the Kingdom of God. Jesus' answer is never found in a leadership class. It is contrary to almost all modern teaching concerning church leadership. *"But Jesus called them to him, and saith unto them, Ye know that they which are accounted to rule over the Gentiles exercise lordship over them; and their great ones exercise authority upon them. But so shall it not be among you: but whosoever will be great among you, shall be your minister: And whosoever of you will be the chiefest, shall be servant of all."* Mark 10:42-44.

Jesus said we could not exercise authority over one another! But the church makes a major doctrine over submitting to authority. We should, no doubt, show respect to those who serve in offices of the church. But, we have one authority, Jesus. His authority is expressed through the written Word. The Lordship of Jesus is the only authority that should reign in our life.

The codependent leader sees authority as a central issue. He must continually have his authority validated. Therefore, serving is no longer the goal, being in control becomes the goal. The head of a ministry has the right (authority) to make all the decisions he feels necessary concerning how he will conduct business, do the work of the ministry, etc., but he has no authority over another person.[2]

People can choose to follow my leadership or not follow my leadership. That is their choice. I only have the right (authority) to do what I do. I must live with their reactions and consequences. They have the right (authority) to do what they will do and they must live with the consequences.

In the codependent church, control is a major issue. Few churches split over any other issue. When different groups start wanting control, there will be a split. The codependent leader tries to justify his control by his intentions. He intends to help the people. He intends to minister to them. If he would look a little deeper, he may find that he needs for them to need him. He needs to be their savior. He needs them to be codependent.

Circumstance theology is a theology that people create in order to justify their circumstances.[3] Out of a need to have control, the codependent leader begins to create theological concepts to justify his position. At this point I must say, when the major issues of a church are not centered around reaching the lost, bringing people into a meaningful relationship with God and equipping (mending) God's people for the work of the ministry, it's starting to get a little far out. There are a lot of other issues, but these are central to the mission of the Church.[4]

The doctrine of "covering", submission, and authority, are completely contrary to Jesus' statement about authority. These doctrines emerged from the concept of control-oriented ministry. When we, as leaders, do not trust the Holy Spirit's ability to work in the hearts of God's people, we feel the need to control. This probably did not come from evil men, it came from compassionate, Christian leaders who did not believe Jesus' teaching about authority and control.

This whole concept says, "If you will submit to me (who is the more spiritual) I will assure that you can stay in God's will. After all, you're not nearly spiritual enough to hear and know God's will." This immediately removes a person from personal responsibility to hear and obey God. This destroys their confidence in God's desire to commune personally with them. This places a man in the position of mediator between God and man. Yet, the Bible says, *"For there is one God, and one mediator between God and men, the man Christ Jesus."* 1 Timothy 2:5.

Even if a man could find the "will of God" for you, he could not empower you with the grace of God to walk it out. You would still be left to your own strength. But the reality is that no man can consistently hear God for another. There may be the rare times that God will speak to someone else in our behalf, but our personal direction should come from the Word of God and the Spirit of God, both working in our own heart.

This doctrine removed the possibility of a healthy relationship of trust and real leadership. It is one thing for people to follow our leadership because we have earned their trust; it is another for them to follow our direction because they think we have the ability to affect God's blessings for them. This concept came straight from the Old Testament, the Catholic Church, and then was adjusted for the Protestant and spiritualized for the Charismatic.

This is a control-motivated, fear-based approach to ministry. When fear is the basis of our actions and decisions, it is not a godly thing. Fear destroys the ability to experience the love of God. The love of God that is being experienced directly affects the level of fear in our life. *"There is no fear in love; but perfect love casteth out fear: because fear hath torment. He that feareth is not made perfect in love."* 1 John 4:18.

The new believer walks into the codependent church and very quickly realizes that this is the same system that works in the world. In order to function here, I must remain carnal-minded. This is the "good ol' boy" system among Christians.

There are many good churches in America and around the world but, there are also many control-oriented churches, led by codependent leaders, that nurture codependent attitudes in people as a way of control.

In my work in other countries, evangelists tell me that tens of thousands of people are being won to the Lord regularly. But, controlling preachers are running the new converts out of the church as fast as the evangelists can win them.

When the church functions on the same system as the world, it is stealing the life away from God's people. It becomes the barrier instead of the provider for people to have a meaningful relationship with God.

Every minister must determine if he will use his gift and the church as a way to help God's people or whether he will use God's people as a way to help himself.[5] How he answers this will determine if he creates an unhealthy codependency on the system or a healthy dependency on God.

Because we view success the way the world does, we seek success the way the world does. We feel that our mission is so important that we can use and abuse the people for our own accomplishment. We have forgotten that the people are the mission. Our churches and ministries exist for the people, not for us.

Real success is helping God's people to become whole through a meaningful relationship with God, so they can do the work of the ministry. Whole people serve God. Whole people live godly lives. Whole people have integrity. But, whole people can rarely be controlled or manipulated.

A successful leader serves God's people. He resists the temptation to use God's people to meet the needs that should be met in his relationship with the Lord. The successful leader understands what Jesus said when He said, *"I have meat that ye know not of. My meat (my success)[6] is to do the will of Him who sent me and to finish His work."* John 4:32,34.

Our success is found in the quality of ministry we provide for our people. Our feeling of success is found in our relationship with the Lord. Our numerical success is the fruit of these two. If we accept the world's definition of success, we will destroy and not build, we will hurt and not help.

[1] Parenthesis mine

[2] *Leadership That Builds People Volume I*, Dr. James B. Richards, Impact Ministries, Huntsville, Alabama

[3] *Taking the Limits Off God*, Dr. James B. Richards, Impact Ministries, Huntsville, Alabama

[4] *Leadership That Builds People Volume II*, Dr. James B. Richards, Impact Ministries, Huntsville, Alabama

[5] *Leadership That Builds People Volume I*, Dr. James B. Richards, Impact Ministries, Huntsville, Alabama

[6] Parenthesis mine

22

THE MAN-CENTERED GOSPEL

The codependent church has developed a man-centered gospel. While using all the New Testament terminology, they have pushed man back under the law. He is still attempting to relate to God on the basis of personal performance, in other words, works righteousness. We believe that Jesus came to save us; we know He is Lord; we know He died for us, but, we still attempt to earn righteousness on the basis of personal performance.

The man-centered gospel places all the burden upon man. This is a burden that man could never handle. The early church struggled with this very problem. The converted Jews did not want to turn loose of the law. It had been the basis of security all their life. In order to maintain this false sense of security, they attempted to require the Gentile converts to be circumcised and obey the law.

When the problem was presented to the elders at Jerusalem, Peter gave the most astute answer. *"Now therefore why tempt ye God, to put a yoke upon the neck of the disciples, which neither our fathers nor we were able to bear?"* Acts 15:10. The patriarchs of the Old Covenant could not bear this load. It didn't work. That's why we needed a new covenant. Why attempt to rebuild what has been torn down in order to find the security that should only be found in God. A fear of trusting God, however, creates the need to put man back at the center of the gospel.

The law had one prevalent weakness. It depended on the performance of men to make them righteousness. *"For what the law could not do, in that it was weak through the flesh, God sending his own Son in the likeness of sinful flesh, and for sin, condemned sin in the flesh."* Romans 8:3. Jesus came to deliver man from the power of sin and to give us the gift of righteousness, because we could not earn it. That was the weakness of the law.

For the codependent, peace with God is based on performance. For the man of faith, peace with God is based on the finished work of Jesus. (Romans 5:1) The codependent puts man at the center of salvation; faith puts Jesus at the center of salvation. The codependent finds security in trusting his own efforts; the man of faith finds security in trusting God.

With man at the center of salvation and our hearts established in law and not grace, we have our paradigm of walking with God set to take us into complete *codependent Christianity.*[1] With this paradigm, every decision that the new believer makes will take him deeper into the man-centered gospel of performance, insecurity and more codependency.

The issue of anointing brings us to another area of extreme codependence. In the Old Testament, individuals received an anointing. The anointing was something that came and left. They were not born again. They were not righteous before God. The anointing could not remain on them. Additionally, they had to sanctify themselves to prepare for the anointing. In other words, they had to make themselves holy enough for God to temporarily place His anointing upon them.

In the New Covenant, Jesus has sanctified us. He has made us holy and blameless before God. The work that He has done prepares us to receive the anointing. Unlike the anointing of the Old Covenant, this anointing is for everyone who is born again. Likewise, it does not come and go, it abides on us.

There is not one teaching in the New Testament about how to receive an additional or more powerful anointing. Conversely, the Bible openly states, *"Now he which stablisheth us with you in Christ, and hath anointed us, is God."* 2 Corinthians 1:21. *"But the anointing which ye have received of him abideth in you, and ye need not that any man teach you: but as the same anointing teacheth you of all things, and is truth, and is no lie, and even as it hath taught you, ye shall abide in him."* 1 John 2:27.

The New Testament speaks of the Anointed One. . .Jesus. He is anointed, we are in Him. What anointing we have is something that we received freely at salvation. What happens through our ministry happens as a result of His anointing. Once again, the Bible places Jesus at the center of our attention. The prevalent teaching about anointing places man at the center. The codependent gains confidence to trust God's power based on performance and subjective feelings. The man of faith has confidence because of the finished work of Jesus and the Word of God.

The whole concept of anointing as it is presently taught places one man above another. It seems to say, "You need me, because I have more of

God than you have. I have something special, something that you don't have. Come to me and get it." It places man in a position to look to another man to receive something that he should receive from God. It places man at the center.

God works through men. God's power is demonstrated through men. But, this can happen in a way that causes men to look at how great Jesus is instead of how great the man is. It can cause us to leave a meeting realizing that God is in us the same way He is in the "man of God." We can feel more confident in God or we can feel less confident. We can feel more equipped or less equipped.

Another aspect of the personal anointing message is that in the end it usually says, "If you'll do what I did, as good as I did it, God will anoint you like He anointed me." or "If you'll let me disciple you, you'll learn the secrets I know." Somehow, man always seem to be at the center, getting the glory. The codependent looks at this and is immediately drawn into a codependent relationship with the man of God instead of into a meaningful relationship with the God of the man.

Much of so-called "ministry" does to the Christian what advertising does to the unsuspecting viewer; it creates a sense of lack. It points to what we don't have instead of what we do have. It creates a feeling that we are somehow not where we ought to be. When the apostle John wrote to the believers he said, "*I have not written unto you because ye know not the truth, but because ye know it, and that no lie is of the truth.*" 1 John 2:21. He didn't attempt to make them feel they were in lack. He wanted them to feel complete and confident in Jesus.

Like the advertiser, the codependent minister

creates the sense of need or lack and then offers the solution, which somehow always places the codependent Christian in an obligatory position. Millions of dollars have been given to ministers with a "special anointing" to get your prayers answered, get your loved ones saved, and get you more anointing. When that doesn't work, there is always one more thing you must do.

The Bible teaching that says, *"You are complete in Him,"* was written to the Colossians because they were being made to feel that they somehow needed something more to protect them from the devil.[2] They thought Jesus just wasn't enough. From the time of the garden until now, Satan has always used the strategy of creating a sense of lack.

Adam had no lack in the garden, yet Satan falsely convinced him that he did. Once he stopped focusing on what he had in God, he felt lack and was led into temptation and destruction. To this very day, Satan continually attempts to refute the simple reality that *"you are complete in Him."* When you stop looking to Him, you will look to someone else. When you look to someone else, the grace of God can no longer empower you to live in victory. When you look at lack, you begin to lack.

The new believer walks into church expecting it to be different. He really expects to experience God. He expects to be empowered and have his life changed. Instead, he is almost immediately robbed of the confidence of what God has done for him. Instead of walking in a simple trust for Jesus and His completed, perfect work, he is given a list of things that he must do to get God to do what He promised in Jesus.

Living in victory is made very difficult and

mystical. The new believer who thought he would
be offered a new life of power and victory is instead
disempowered and offered the opportunity to
exchange his past addiction for some new religious
addiction that will offer him only a mere substitute
of the security that could be found in trusting the
finished work of Jesus.

The man-centered gospel places man at the
center. It moves us to look to a man instead of God.
In the end, however, man will always fail and
disappoint us. Unfortunately, we think God has
failed. Our ability to trust God is further
diminished, pushing us deeper into codependency.

[1] I realize this is a contradiction in terms. I use this to
describe the Christian is caught in the trap of religious
codependency.

[2] *The Expositor's Bible Commentary, Volume 11*,
Zondervan Publishing House; Grand Rapids, Michigan

23

ANGRY GOD

Of all the things that create codependent tendencies in a believer, there is probably nothing more destructive than the "angry God" doctrines. The "angry God" doctrines focus in on God's wrath. They make Him appear to be hard to please, hard to understand, difficult to know, and reluctant to communicate.

Most of the "angry God" doctrines come out of the Old Covenant. Under the Old Covenant, sin had not been dealt with, the penalty for sin had not been paid, and man had not been given the free gift of righteousness. Was God angry? Certainly! Definitely! Without question!

Did God change from the Old to the New Covenant? NO! *"For I am the LORD, I change not; therefore ye sons of Jacob are not consumed."* Malachi 3:6. *"Every good gift and every perfect gift is from above, and cometh down from the Father of lights, with whom is no variableness, neither shadow of turning."* James 1:17. God has never, and will never, change. The question then becomes, how do you reconcile the wrath of God in the Old Covenant with mercy and love of the New Covenant?

Simple! God is a holy God. His holiness and righteousness requires that sin be paid for in the body of the sinner. Yet, He is a loving Father who has never wanted to punish man. He has always wanted fellowship and communion with man. But righteousness required that sin be punished. God did that by allowing Jesus to become a man. Man brought sin into the world; a man had to take sin out of the world.

Jesus lived a sinless life. Had He not done so, He would not have qualified to be our sacrifice. When He went to the cross, God made Him to become our sin. All of the wrath of God was appeased, satisfied completely in Jesus.[1] Likewise, all the requirements of righteousness were satisfied. *"For Christ is the end of the law for righteousness to every one that believeth."* Romans 10:4.

Now all of the love that God desired to express to man could be legally given without violating truth, justice, or righteousness. This work of Jesus clearly expresses and declares God's extreme love for man. This is the place where peace was made between God and man, once and for all.

This work is consummated in the life of the believer who receives Jesus as Lord, Savior, and righteousness. Unfortunately, very few people are told that Jesus is their righteousness. As a matter of fact, it is almost as if it has been deliberately hidden. Those who don't believe in the power of righteousness are afraid you won't live right if you find out about the gift of righteousness in Jesus. So instead, they cut you off from the power to live and walk in the righteousness that God has freely given.

The "angry God" message denies everything that Jesus accomplished at the cross. *"Much more then, being now justified by his blood, we shall be saved from wrath through him."* Romans 5:9. The "angry God" message puts enmity between God and man. It makes God appear to be the angry God who must be appeased by our sacrifices. God didn't need the sacrifices of the Old Covenant, nor does He need our sacrifices. The price has been paid. There is no more sacrifice for sin. When we do not accept and trust in the finished work of Jesus, we live in the fear of wrath and judgment which shall devour the adversary. Because we assume ourselves to be adversaries, we feel like adversaries, alone and afraid.

The concept of an angry God puts man into the throes of codependent thinking. He cannot get his needs met from God, therefore, he must look elsewhere. But he wants God. The next best alternative is religion. Thus, you have the makings of a denomination.

Basically, the different denominations and religions are people who have come together and made lists of what they think it will take to make a person righteous and acceptable to God. Every group has their list of requirements. The ignorant and unlearned look over the list to see which one makes sense to them. They want to know which one will make them feel the most secure and that's the one they choose.

Now that they have found the doctrine that makes them secure, they must protect that doctrine. It's sort of like building an idol and calling it your god. Even though you call it your god, you have to protect it so no one can steal it and use it for fire wood. Some god, huh?

The reason people become so dogmatic and argumentative about their doctrine, is because it is their security. When you cause them to question their doctrine, you are causing them to question the security of their salvation. It is no wonder people become so closed and defensive.

The man of faith believes and then experiences the truth. He accepts Jesus on His terms. He believes and trusts God more than he trusts his own logic and reason. Because he is not trusting a myth, he has the opportunity to experience the person behind the truth. His experience goes far beyond the intellectual concept that must be argued and protected. It is in a person, Jesus.

Truth is not the reality, it only represents and expresses the reality. The Word of God is truth and it expresses many realities. Until we leave the realm of truth and enter the realm of experiencing that truth, we are not dealing with Jesus, we are simply embracing the portrait the Word presents of Him. The man of faith is not content to live in the realm of information. Even if the information is correct, it is still merely information.

Jesus never said that merely knowing the truth would set you free. He said if you continue in it, or put it into practice, then you will know it experientially. Then when you experience it, it will set you free. " *Then said Jesus to those Jews which believed on him, If ye continue in my word, then are ye my disciples indeed; And ye shall know the truth, and the truth shall make you free.*" John 8:31-32.

The man of faith allows that truth to draw him into a relationship with God through Jesus, based on truth. The codependent, on the other hand, who is too fearful to have a meaningful relationship with a man much less with God, draws back and embraces the information, never entering into the realm of experience and freedom. The concept of an angry God presents a picture of fear and rejection that is too overwhelming for the codependent to face.

If you are not righteous through Jesus, you must earn your righteousness. Based on the level of righteousness that you earn, you will be acceptable to God. That is the subtle, unspoken message behind the codependent gospel, which is no gospel (good news) at all. This puts man in the most extreme emotional stress he could ever endure. You are not, therefore, you must become.

Every religion in the world tries to get you to become by doing. Christianity, however, says you can do because you have become. You can live righteous because you are righteous. You can be happy because you have joy. You can be at ease because you have peace. You can enter into rest because you are accepted. There are over two hundred scriptures in the New Testament that tell us who we are, in Jesus.[2]

The codependent leader who desperately needs to be needed, tells us who we are not. He tells us how much we lack. He tells us what we do not have. The man of faith tells us who we are, what we can do, and what we have because of the finished work of Jesus. He doesn't make us feel like needy beggars. He makes us feel like a priest and a king.

1 *The Gospel of Peace*, Dr. James B. Richards, Impact Ministries, Huntsville, Alabama

2 *The Prayer Organizer*, Dr. James B. Richards, Impact Ministries, Huntsville, Alabama

24

THE MESSAGE OF FAITH

One of the greatest potential messages to come down the gospel highway in years, has been the message of faith. Like anything with great potential for good, there is also great potential for harm when this message falls into the domain of the codependent leader. No matter how great the truth, the codependent will always manipulate the message for personal validation.

When I first began to hear the faith message, it was as pure as the driven snow. For the first time, I heard people preach many of the things I had believed and preached. It was such a confirmation. In the beginning, there was much emphasis on the finished work of Jesus, faith righteousness, and the goodness of God.

Like every movement, though, the followers don't have the heart of the leaders. Codependency crept in, and in less than a decade, a message that had so much potential to heal, began to bring forth its potential for harm. Like every good thing, the potential for detraction (diminish, lessen, reduce) is present at its conception.

The first trouble sign was the apparent lack of emphasis on a relationship with Jesus. Obviously, many of the original leaders had strong, meaningful relationships with the Lord that empowered their faith. True to form, however, as the codependent followers assimilated the message of faith, they left out the relationship with God and kept the formulas. Before long, the emphasis on God and His faithfulness had been pushed aside for the message of how much man had to do to get God to respond. It had become man-centered.

The message of faith has very subtly changed from our response of trust to what God has done, to how we can get God to respond by what we can do. The man-centered message of works crept in, and perverted the message, and robbed it of its power. What once glorified God, now glorified the faith of man.

The very first foundation of the faith is *"repentance from dead works."* Hebrews 6:1. The dead works he mentions is not all of the sinful things that he did before he got saved. It was all of the religious things he did to earn God's approval. Under the law, man did things to try to get God to respond. Under the New Covenant, God did everything in Jesus. He now gives us the opportunity to respond to what He has done. Faith is a response of trust.

Unbelief responds by de-emphasizing what God has done and placing the burden to perform back on man. It places man at the center. Otherwise, the codependent would have to trust God and His integrity.

By the message of faith being twisted to what we must do to get God to respond, we come up with all manner of wrong questions. How much faith does it take to get God to move? How can I make my faith stronger? How long do I have to believe? Why isn't God doing anything? Is sin blocking my faith?

In all of Jesus' teaching about faith, He never

emphasized how much it took, as much as He emphasized how little it took. Our problem with God is rarely a lack of faith, as much as it is the abundance of unbelief. Every man has a measure of faith. We believed God for the greatest miracle that would ever happen with infant faith; we got born again. God changed our very nature. There is no miracle any greater. Why should anything else require more faith?

In some circles, the proof that you had faith became the amount of "stuff" you had. If you had a lot of stuff, you must obviously have a lot of faith. Getting the stuff, so you could prove you had faith, became more important than knowing and serving God. For many, what had originally been presented as trusting and walking with God, became an attempt to get a lot of "stuff" so you wouldn't need God. Security came when a person was convinced he had enough faith to get all the "stuff" he wanted.

Once again, codependent people twisted truth and de-emphasized a meaningful relationship with God. Security was found in the amount of faith one could prove that one had. The codependent heart will pervert and twist any message away from God, to a place of dependency on other things.

With this twist, the standard answer for every problem simply became, "You don't have enough faith." Once again, the emphasis was placed on what you don't have in Jesus, instead of what you do have. Man was once again made to be incomplete and inadequate.

Remember, one of the basic goals of the codependent is control. When he is in control, he feels secure. Therefore, the codependent leader always seeks to disempower others. If others can somehow be convinced of their lack, then they will need the codependent leader. He will be in control and he will be secure. All of this will be justified by the legitimate needs that exist in the people.

The man of faith would approach those needs with an emphasis on your ability to handle and solve these problems because of Christ in you. While he would lovingly point out the problem, he would not tell you that you were not righteous. Like Paul, he would tell you to *"walk worthy of your calling"* or *"yield your members to righteousness."* Or as Peter said, *"Seeing then that all these things shall be dissolved, what manner of persons ought ye to be in all holy conversation and godliness."* 2 Peter 3:11. Even when Paul wrote the Corinthian church and rebuked them for their apparent carnality, he reminded them of their righteousness. *"But of him are ye in Christ Jesus, who of God is made unto us wisdom, and righteousness, and sanctification, and redemption."* 1 Corinthians 1:30. *"For he hath made him to be sin for us, who knew no sin; that we might be made the righteousness of God in him."* 2 Corinthians 5:21. *"Be ye not unequally yoked together with unbelievers: for what fellowship hath righteousness with unrighteousness? and what communion hath light with darkness?"* 2 Corinthians 6:14.

The man of faith would never move you to take your eyes off Jesus and His finished work. He would desire that you trust in and depend on the power of God. The codependent would always have you take your eyes off Jesus and look, instead, to your need, and ultimately to him as the one who will help you meet your need.

I have found that it does not matter what the message is. The codependent will pervert it into something that gives him control. In the early 60's and 70's, as people were baptized in the Holy Spirit and leaving the denominational churches, there was the realization that people needed to be discipled. This is a truth. The Bible tells us to make disciples of all men.

Regardless of the sincerity of those early leaders, this movement ended up totally revolving around control. What started out as people being discipled unto Jesus, became people being disciples of other people. The grace of God working in our heart gave way to the power of men working on our mind. For the carnal, insecure leader, this became the justification to control. One man would make another man godly by discipling him. How utterly codependent!

The same thing has happened with the prophesy movement. What started out as an attempt to restore a precious gift to the body of Christ, became a method to control and dominate the lives of the people. When a church member does anything that displeases leadership, that displeasure can always be expressed as a word from the Lord. The New Testament believer then begins to consult the prophet instead of consulting God.

The codependent tries to turn every great phenomenon into something that every person should do. If you are not involved in what I am involved in, you're going to miss the last great move of God. Or, if you don't do what I'm doing, you are in rebellion to God. The codependent insists that everyone have all of the same experiences that he has. This validates him and his experience. Think of it, Jesus never had a movement. He ministered to every person differently. It never happened the same way twice. There wasn't a "spit in the mud and rub on your sickness" movement. There wasn't a "wash in the pool" movement.

Jesus ministered to every person individually. He yielded to the Holy Spirit as He led Him to minister in specific ways. Jesus was not committed to a method, He was committed to God and to people. He didn't need for everyone to approve of His method. His validation came from His relationship with the Father, not from the approval of man or the size of the crowd.

"Faith worketh by love!" The real man of faith is established in the love of God. His roots go deep into the soil of love. His confidence is not in how much faith he has, but in how much love God has. He knows that God is good and that He is faithful. He knows that trusting God's love is the key. As Paul prayed in Ephesians, *"That he would grant you, according to the riches of his glory, to be strengthened with might by his Spirit in the inner man; That Christ may dwell in your hearts by faith; that ye, being rooted and grounded in love, May be able to comprehend with all saints what is the breadth, and length, and depth, and height; And to know the love of Christ, which passeth knowledge, that ye might be filled with all the fulness of God."* Ephesians 3:16-19.

Being filled with the fullness of God is a matter of faith. Not a matter of how much faith one has, but a matter of what he has faith in. Faith in the love of God causes us to be filled with the fullness of God.

SECTION 4: THE CURE

SECTION 4:
INTRODUCTION

Without a cure this book would simply be another "you ought to" book that made you feel inadequate and less than capable. But, I offer you a cure that is simple. It is so simple that it has been overlooked, doubted, and rejected for hundreds of years. Have a relationship with God through the Lord Jesus!

Run the risk. Meet God on His own terms. Put aside all of your fears and doubts, and enter into a place that few people choose to go. Enter into the place that people sing about, pray about, write poems about, preach sermons about, but seldom enter in. Enter into the love of the Father.

It may take you years to read and incorporate the following chapters into your life. Not because it will be hard or difficult, but because it will involve a lifetime of walking with God. It is a never-ending process of believing, experiencing, and growing in your confidence of the love of God.

A relationship is not a destination; it is a process. Thus, it must be continually updated, renewed, and allowed to undergo change and growth. You will spend all of this life and eternity growing in your relationship with God. Begin now; make Him the center of your life.

25

DIGNITY AND WORTH

The level of a person's self-worth will control everything he does. It will determine how he interprets all of the information he ever hears. It will effect the amount and quality of effort he puts into anything. Self-worth is one of the deepest needs of a human being. Our sense of dignity and worth determines if we will steal or work for the things we desire. It determines if we will lie or tell the truth to gain favor. Man always seeks to fulfill his desires in a way that is consistent with his self-perception.

In Hebrews 2:7 it says that God originally crowned man with glory and honor. These words *glory* and *honor* include the concept of dignity and worth. In the beginning, man walked and ruled planet earth from the sense of dignity and worth. His sense of identity and worth came from his relationship to the Father. He knew who he was in relation to God.

After the fall, man lost his sense of dignity because now he felt afraid of God. He hid in shame from the One who previously met his every need. Fear replaced love. Shame replaced honor. Cowardice drove out confidence. Unbelief consumed faith. Fear and shame led to sinful actions, which further confirmed these negative emotions. Thus, you have the destructive cycle of low self-worth. Negative feelings and low evaluation of self leads to actions consistent with that low evaluation. Those actions bring about more negative feelings, which bring about more negative actions.

Being born-again does not automatically break this cycle. There are actually churches that nurture low self-worth as if it had some inherent value. What will change this cycle is the renewing of the mind. Paul exhorted the Ephesians to *"walk not as other Gentiles walk in the vanity of their mind."* Ephesians 4:17. He told the Romans, *"be ye transformed by the renewing of your mind."* Romans 12:2. He told the Corinthians to *"cast down **imaginations**, and every high thing that exalteth itself against the knowledge of God, and bringing into captivity every **thought** to the obedience of Christ."* 2 Corinthians 10:5. The real warfare that the New Testament presents for the believer is bringing his thoughts and beliefs in line with the New Covenant. To be born-again and continue to think the same, will bring little change.

Man's sense of dignity and worth is only restored when he fully accepts the terms and conditions of the New Covenant. Dignity and worth are restored because our loving, peaceful relationship with God is restored. As we experience acceptance from God as our Father, we have a restoration of identity. As we experience God's love and value for us, we establish our sense of self-worth. As we realize the true image of God, we develop a new image of ourselves. [1]

We have been adopted into the family of God. We have been given a new nature, a new identity. We are made completely righteous before God. Because we are in Jesus, we are as righteous as He is. These are the terms of the new covenant. This is the covenant that Jesus established for us. We must accept these terms.

Unbelief causes us to look back to the performance mentality of the Old Covenant and we try to mix the two. We are simply afraid to believe that God is so good and so loving that He would have made us such an offer. That unbelief is exactly what is our problem.

Even when someone comes to believe that God is good, they may still reject the idea that we are qualified to be the recipients of that goodness apart from works. Paul said, "*. . .the Father. . . hath made us meet to be partakers of the inheritance of the saints in light.*" Colossians 1:12. The NIV translates the word *meet* as *qualified.* God made us qualified to receive the inheritance. We can't qualify ourselves. All that we need to function in this new covenant is freely given in Jesus! And we are qualified in Jesus! There is nothing left to do, but believe and receive.

We are no longer the same person we were, but we must renew our minds to see ourselves and think of ourselves in light of this transformation. We should not allow one thought or imagination about ourselves to emerge that is inconsistent with who we are in Jesus. When those thoughts or imaginations do emerge, we should not entertain them.

As the realization of righteousness becomes the foundation of our self-perception, our self-worth will be restored to the New Testament reality. When we see ourselves the way God sees us, we will experience the power to live life the way God says we can. When we believe we are righteous, the power of righteousness will flow out of our spirit into every aspect of our being.

It only takes a few weeks to establish a habit and a few more weeks for that habit to become second nature.[2] If a person simply devoted a few weeks of taking control of their thoughts, the rest of their life would change. A few weeks of directing every thought to the realities of the New Covenant would transform your self-worth. You would no longer see yourself as the sum total of your life's actions; you would see yourself as righteous, sanctified, anointed, and qualified in Jesus.

It is not what you stop that will change your life, it is what you start. An attempt to stop thinking the wrong thoughts would be tormenting and self-defeating. The key is thinking the right thoughts. There are a few basic things you can do to transform your thought life. You must decide which method will work for you.

When I first began the process of establishing my thoughts in the finished work of Jesus, I developed what I now call *The Prayer Organizer*.[3] My prayer organizer was a system where I organized hundreds of identity scriptures into topics that related to the promises and nature of God. I would spend time daily acknowledging and worshipping God from these scriptures.

The first thirty minutes of the morning and the last thirty minutes of the evening are the times that the sub-conscious mind[4] is the most receptive. Therefore, I would use those times to renew my mind. In the morning, I would spend time verbally acknowledging scripture. In the evening, I would spend time meditating on scripture.

I never turned this into a legalistic ritual. I knew I was not trying to become what the scripture said. I was not trying to get God to do something, I was simply renewing my mind. The wrong motivation could make this or any other scriptural endeavor a legalistic nightmare.

During the day, if I found myself thinking thoughts that were not consistent with who God said I was, I would deal with those thoughts. I would bring those thoughts captive to the obedience of Christ. I always went back to what Jesus had accomplished by His finished work. I refused to see myself in any way other than how God has made me; in Him.

As the years have gone by, I have found myself spending less and less time doing any of these things. I no longer have the need. My new identity is written on my heart and my mind. I no longer act in a base way. I no longer have negative feelings about myself. I no longer wonder if I am qualified. I have a sense of identity, self-image, and self-worth that is based on the finished work of Jesus. My actions and emotions are empowered by believing the truth.

I am not who you say I am. I am not who my circumstances say I am. I am not even who my actions say I am. I **am** who God says I am. He says I am a righteous son, because of the finished work of Jesus.

Out of this new identity in Jesus flows a new sense of dignity and worth. Dignity and worth guide my emotions and my decisions. They provide me with consistent emotional stability.

It is my opinion that dignity and worth are the essential foundations for a healthy emotional life and meaningful relationships with God and man.

[1] *My Church My Family*, Dr. James B. Richards, Impact Ministries, Huntsville, Alabama

[2] *Competent to Counsel*, Jay Adams, Baker Book House, Grand Rapids Michigan

[3] *The Prayer Organizer,* Dr. James B. Richards, Impact Ministries, Huntsville, Alabama

[4] In my opinion, the sub-conscious mind is what the Bible identifies as the heart.

26

PEACE WITH GOD

Accepting righteousness as a free gift in Jesus, puts your heart at rest. You never have to wonder where you stand with God. *"If your heart condemns you, God is greater than your heart."* 1 John 3:20. Knowing who you are and what you have become, gives complete peace with God. (Romans 5:1)

Peace is far more essential to living than we think. Our works mentality places all the emphasis on being right. Being right means proving I am right. Proving I am right means proving you are wrong. Proving you are wrong means conflict. Our entire approach to Christianity has been one that has robbed us of peace with God and man. Instead of giving us peace, it has placed us in the throws of insecurity and conflict.

Peace is only found in the absence of striving. Striving to become steals peace. Accepting that "I am" in Jesus, establishes peace. *"Be careful for nothing; but in every thing by prayer and supplication with thanksgiving let your requests be made known unto God. And the peace of God, which passeth all understanding, shall keep your hearts and minds through Christ Jesus."* Philippians 4:7.

We tend to turn this verse around and say, "If I will keep my mind, then I can have peace." But, it actually says that if I keep peace by trusting God, peace will keep my heart and my mind. So, I should make the peace of God a top priority in my life. I can personally remember when I came to the place where I had value for peace. When I made peace a priority, many others factors came into line.

When we think of peace, there are many concepts that come to mind. Let's see if we can bring all of these concepts together into a Biblical understanding of peace. The New Testament word for *peace* is a very inclusive word. It involves a tranquility of mind, but fortunately, it does not stop there. The word for *peace* in the New Testament is very similar to the word s*halom* in the Old Testament. It speaks of tranquility in relationships and tranquility of mind. It speaks of completeness, wholeness, and prosperity.

A person could have a tranquil state of mind, simply because they were deceived. In others words, it was a false, circumstantial peace. People will often inform me of unbiblical decisions they have made. When I point out that their decision is inconsistent with scripture, their defense is, "Well, I know it's of God because I have peace." Then I have to ask if they know the difference between relief and peace. Peace that is not based on truth is deceitful. It may give a measure of relief, but be assured that relief will disappear and give way to negative emotions.

The peace of God, however, is a tranquility that is based on reality. It has substance. It is a tranquility that comes, first and foremost, from believing that there is peace between you and God. Often times, the first thought to attack us when things go wrong is, "What did I do to cause God to allow this?" That is what the Bible calls condemnation. Our first response to those kinds of vain imaginations must be, "There is peace between God and me, because I am in Jesus."

James says it this way, *"Let no man say when he is tempted (tested, tried, scrutinized), I am tempted (tested, tried, scrutinized) of God: for God cannot be tempted with evil, neither tempteth (tests, tries, scrutinizes) he any man."* James 1:13. When we think it is God testing us, we are not in faith and therefore, we cannot have peace. God teaches, guides, directs, empowers, and comforts by the Holy Spirit. He is not the spirit of destruction, He is the Spirit of Life.

In the Book of Colossians, Paul says, *"And, having made peace through the blood of his cross, by him to reconcile all things unto himself; by him, I say, whether they be things in earth, or things in heaven. And you, that were sometime alienated and enemies in your mind by wicked works, yet now hath he reconciled In the body of his flesh through death, to present you holy and unblameable and unreproveable in his sight."* Colossians 1:22. Because God has made peace with us through Jesus, He presents us to Himself holy and blameless. He has no basis of reproving us.

If we are not holy enough for God, it is His problem. He made us holy. He made us righteous. Why would He make us righteous and then criticize us? He wouldn't. *"Who shall lay any thing to the charge of God's elect? God that justifieth? Who is he that condemneth? Christ that died, yea rather, that is risen again, who is even at the right hand of God, who also maketh intercession for us?"* Romans 8:34.[1] Paul is asking a simple question. Is the God that justified you going to bring a charge against you? No! Is the Savior that died and rose again for you going to condemn you? No! God is not schizophrenic. If He criticizes your righteousness, He is criticizing His own handiwork. That would be like God criticizing the stars and blaming us. Why would He blame us? We didn't make them. Likewise, we didn't make ourselves righteous, we accepted it as a free gift. If our righteousness is not perfect, then neither is Jesus' righteousness, because the righteousness we have is His. If it is not good enough to bring us before God, then Jesus cannot come before God.

This peace we have is also based on the fact that we have completeness in Jesus. *"We have everything that pertains unto life and godliness through the knowledge of Him."* 2 Peter 1:3. I have more than mere tranquility, I have tranquility that is based on the fact that I have all I need for life and godliness. I need not be troubled nor worried if I have enough faith to get God to give me something, there is nothing left for Him to give me. I have it all in Jesus.

I may not be experiencing all that I need at this moment, but I need not be concerned that this is an indication something is wrong between God and myself. I need not be concerned that I am lacking enough faith or righteousness. There may be problems in my life that I must deal with and there may sin in my life that should be conquered, but I can face that without fear of separation from God. As Paul said in Romans 8:35-39, can any of these things separate us from the love of God that is in Jesus? No! None of these can separate us from His love. There is not one place in the New Testament that tells me my sin can separate me from God. Does this mean that it's all right to continue in sin? No!

The thing that makes us acceptable to God, is the fact that we have been made righteous in Jesus. This is the good news (gospel) of Jesus. The good news is not that you could go to heaven when you die. The Old Covenant believers looked confidently to eternity with God. The good news is not that there would be healings or miracles, they had seen healing and miracles in the Old Covenant. The good news is: I will give you righteousness as a free gift. If you're tired and worn out from religion, come to me and I will give you rest to your soul.

"Therefore if any man be in Christ, he is a new creature: old things are passed away; behold, all things are become new." 2 Corinthians 5:17. We are not a cleaned up version of who we were, we are a totally new creation, a perfectly righteous creation. We can stroll right into the holy of holies with no fear of falling over dead. We can stand before God unashamed. We can *"come boldly before the throne of grace"* because there is peace between us and God. Sin has been punished, wrath has been appeased, and righteousness has been given.

I must cling to the reality that there is peace between God and me because of Jesus. I must have my feet shod with a readiness of mind that comes from a thorough preparation in the gospel of peace. I must cling to peace. Peace will keep my heart and my mind stable. Peace will keep me stable in a way that I don't even understand.

This peace with God keeps me at the place where I can experience all the good things of God. My faith is functional to the degree that I believe the gospel of peace.[2] (Romans 10:13-17) I can experience tranquility based on the fact that there is peace with God and He has given me all I need for life and godliness.

[1] I removed the italicized words to add clarity. The words *"It is"* are not in the original text.

[2] ***The Gospel of Peace,*** Dr. James B. Richards, Impact Ministries, Huntsville, Alabama

27

EXPERIENCING GOD

Nothing has any value in this life, unless it is experienced in this life. To be saved will definitely benefit us in eternity, but if being saved does not benefit us in this life, it is of no value now. Being righteous is a wonderful thing, but if I am not empowered to live righteous, my life will still be filled with destruction. We should experience God here and now so we will benefit in this life.

Through the years, faith has been interpreted and viewed in many different perspectives. Today, faith is taught as a force that we release to get things to happen. But there was a time when we were taught that faith was when you believed in something that you could not prove or experience, you just took it by faith. Neither of those interpretations are correct and both lead to problems. It is the latter concept we shall look at.

Man has consistently developed circumstance theology throughout the years. When he is not experiencing what the Bible says he should experience, man has developed a theology to justify himself and protect his ego. It was not many years after the death of Jesus that the church backslid. A relationship with Jesus was replaced with a relationship with the church. People were no longer encouraged to know God personally, nor even read the Bible for themselves. That was reserved for the clergy. They would know God and read the Bible and pass it all along to you.

We know that the real goal here was control, but that control would have never been possible if man had maintained a meaningful relationship with God. Many began to accept doctrine "by faith." They accepted that it was true, although they never experienced any power from what they believed.

The Bible says, *"The gospel is the power of God unto salvation."* Romans 1:16. If what we are believing has no power in it, it is not gospel. Or, if we are hearing the gospel and we do not believe it, it will not have power in our life. But if we hear and believe the gospel, it will have the power to bring us into salvation.

The Greek word for salvation is *sozo.* Sozo means to be saved, healed, delivered, blessed, prospered, made whole, set apart, and a lot more. It has to do with a salvation in this life. Not so much a change in circumstances, as a change in us. Our heart and emotions change. We now have the power to win over the circumstances, whether they change or not.

The ability to prosper and be in good health is directly related to something happening to us in the realm of the soul. *"Beloved, I wish above all things that thou mayest prosper and be in health, even as thy soul prospereth."* 3 John 1:2. Salvation should not only affect our spirit, it must also affect our soul, which is our mind, emotions, and will.

For years, we have been afraid to deal with the issue of feelings and emotions. Because of the extremes of some groups who give themselves over to emotions, we have rejected the validity of emotions all together. Regardless of whether you believe it or not, your emotions are a major factor in what is controlling your life.

You are a living soul. You experience life in the soul. The soul is neither good nor evil, it is simply the place where you experience the emotional effects of good and evil. Every battle you fight, every bad thing that controls you, every good thing that brings you joy, does so because it affects your soul. Like it or not, you live out of your feelings.

Emotions follow thinking. It is universally agreed that the soul is the place of the mind, the emotions, and the will. The mind is where we think. These thoughts produce emotions. These emotions affect our will, our ability to make decisions and see them through. The will determines our actions.

We should not be led by our emotions, but we should know how to lead our emotions. Unbiblical thinking produces unbiblical emotions. The feeling of low self-worth is the product of thinking and believing certain things about yourself. Hatred is an emotion that is based on thoughts and beliefs. Joy is an emotion based on thoughts and beliefs.

Our momentary thoughts produce momentary emotions that come and go. Our habitual thoughts produce beliefs that reside in our heart and direct our life without conscious thought. Thoughts that become beliefs produce constant emotions. These emotions dictate our every decision.

Thinking Biblical thoughts produces corresponding emotions of life, peace, and joy. If we don't think what the Bible says, we will never believe what the Bible says, therefore, we will never experience what the Bible says. Accepting the fact that God loves us, believing that we have been made righteous, and thereby, have peace with God, produces feelings of dignity and worth.

The apostle John put it this way, *"And we have known and believed the love that God hath to us. God is love."* 1 John 4:16. First they believed the love of God. Then they *knew* (the Greek word here is *gnosko* and means experienced) the love of God. They didn't merely accept the fact that God loved them, they believed it. It became a part of their thinking. They ultimately began to feel His love.

One of the greatest changes in my life is when I began to feel the love of God on a continual basis. Much of my life I felt anger. The earliest strong emotion I can remember was hatred. I wanted to kill my father. I would lay awake at night when I was only four or five years old and plan to kill him. I can remember thinking, "If I can stay awake until he goes to sleep, I can sneak into the kitchen, get a knife, and kill him in his sleep." I hated him.

I carried the feeling of hatred and anger in me all of my childhood and teenage years. I was angry with others because that is what I was experiencing in my own soul. The way we relate to others is always a reflection of what we are currently experiencing. Christians who believe in works righteousness always feel rejected. Therefore, they reject others. If they feel that God looks for fault, they look for fault. Whatever we are presently experiencing is what we pour onto others.[1]

"Beloved, let us love one another: for love is of God; and every one that loveth is born of God, and knoweth God. He that loveth not knoweth not God; for God is love." 1 John 4:7-8. Everyone that loves knoweth (is experiencing) God. He that loveth not, knoweth not (is not experiencing) God.

When we begin to experience love, we will feel

loved. Nearly every morning when I awaken, I feel the love of God. It is an emotion that is based on a belief that is based on the reality. It is confirmed by the Word of God and expressed by the Spirit of God. This is more than a feeling that is generated by a thought. It is that and more. It is a feeling that is based on experiencing God.

To experience God, one must enter into a personal relationship with Him. You will have to find comfortable ways to spend time together. You will have to learn of Him. It is a relationship. Having a relationship with God is not as difficult or as mystical as we have been led to believe. He wants to commune with you. He is for you, not against you. He did all that He did in Jesus because of His love for you. He wants you to believe His love, but He also wants you to feel His love.

Reading the Bible, prayer, and worship can be dry and legalistic, or it can be full of life. Your intention is what makes the difference. If you are just doing your religious duties, it will have no life. If, on the other hand, you are entering into a personal relationship with God, it will be full of life.

I always experience God when I pray, read the Bible, or worship. I don't want to learn about Him, I want to know Him. He is always ready to know you and commune with you.

The scripture that says, *"Behold I stand at the door and knock. . ."* was not written to the lost, it was written to the church that had closed Him out of their heart. They had religion, but they were no longer experiencing God, personally.

[1] ***Knowing and Feeling the Love of God*** Audio Tape Series, Dr. James B. Richards, Impact Ministries, Huntsville, Alabama

28

COMMITMENT TO LOVE

Even though I am righteous because of the finished work of Jesus, that righteousness will benefit me nothing if I do not walk in it. In all of Paul's writing, he would spend chapters pointing out who we were in Jesus or teaching about our righteousness in Him. After being sure that we understood our relationship with God, he would then talk to us about the way we lived.

It is essential that we live according to our new nature. This does not earn us anything with God, but it does affect our ability to relate to Him. It also has a great effect on every other relationship, as well as our own self-perception.

Luke 6:38 says, *"Give, and it shall be given unto you; good measure, pressed down, and shaken together, and running over, shall men give into your bosom. For with the same measure that ye mete withal it shall be measured to you again."* This verse has traditionally been used to teach about money, but Jesus is talking about how we relate to people. He is saying, if we judge, people will give judgment back to us. If we are merciful, people will give mercy back to us. Whatever we give others is exactly what they will give back to us. With one addition, they are going to multiply it when they give it back.[1]

God is able to love perfectly and continuously,

but people are not. With people, you will reap what you sow. You will continue to experience pain and rejection in your relationships if you are not committed to walking in love. You will destroy any opportunity for a meaningful, loving relationship. You will create all of the scenarios that pushed you so far into codependency.

By entering into a relationship with the Lord that is personal and intimate, you will grow in the love of God. You will begin to experience His love and you will find the source of your emotional needs. As you experience God's love, you will become more equipped, more capable of walking in love toward others. Most of what we demonstrate to others is simply a reflection of what we are experiencing in our own life.

One of the most interesting things about our personal development is what I call "growth on parallel planes." What is happening in one area of our life is always reflected in other areas. Sometimes it is not only reflected in other areas, sometimes it is a reflection of other areas. Likewise, as we experience something on one plane, it always affects us on another plane.

For example, when people go through relationship problems, it is common for them to harden their heart against the other person. This is a means of protection, a way to keep from getting hurt. When we harden our heart against someone, our heart also hardens against God. What we thought would only affect us on this plane, begins to affect us on the spiritual plane as well. Likewise, when a person hardens their heart to the Lord, it begins to affect the way they treat people. So, growth or destruction tends to happen on parallel planes.

1 John 4:12 says, *"No man hath seen God at any time. If we love one another, God dwelleth in us, and his love is perfected in us."* God's love is perfected in us as we walk in love one to another. The word *perfect* means to be brought to the goal or to reach completion. First of all, if God's love doesn't move us into loving relationships with others, it is not accomplishing the goal. God has never intended that we would be the recipients of His love simply for our personal pleasure or experience. It is not supposed to stop with us. It is supposed to be multiplied through us.

We are to be the channel through which the world sees and experiences God until they can see and experience Him for themselves. The world can't see God, but they can see us. Many times the Christian is so hurt they can't see God, but they can see us. As others experience the love of God through us, we can multiply love and peace in the world the same way rejection and codependency has been multiplied.

Likewise, as we walk in love toward others, the love of God grows in us. We become able to experience His love in a more real way. Loving others does not make Him love us more. We are not earning the right to experience His love. Rather, we are developing the capacity to experience love.

God has always loved us with a perfect love. He has always wanted us to experience His love. What has lacked, is our capacity to experience love. Even though He has always been giving, we have not always been receiving. The problem has never been His capacity to give love, it has been in our capacity to receive love.

As we receive the grace of God to walk in love toward others, that capacity to give love expands our capacity to receive love. Not only do we grow on parallel planes, we always grow bi-dimensionally. The grace (capacity & ability) to give love always brings the grace (capacity & ability) to receive love. The Psalmist said, *"I will run the way of thy commandments, when thou shalt enlarge my heart."* Psalms 119:32. He knew he must be enlarged in his heart to have the capacity to *"run the way of the commandments."*

A part of what has rendered us incapable of experiencing God's love, is the way we have withheld love or misused love in the past. We have reaped what we have sown. Our own heart has been affected by the way we treat others. It is difficult to believe in unconditional love when we only give conditional love. It is hard to believe in mercy when we are unmerciful.

As we love others, however, the love of God is perfected in us. That love of God that we pour out of our heart, heals our own heart. In every way, our capacity for love is expanded as we expand our capacity to give love. We must, therefore, remove all guile from our expressions of love. We must not use kindness as a means to manipulate. We must commit ourselves to the love of God and keep our motives in check.

Among the first and most primary decisions, is the release of control. Whether we are the aggressive or passive controller, we must give up control. We must honestly face the pain that is brought into the lives of others and our own lives through our attempts to control.

There is often great value in having an honest discussion with those around us to make them aware of our intention to release them from our control. It is important to receive their forgiveness.

Once the people around us are aware that we really intend to release them from our control, we may have to face things that we've never been willing to face. But with confidence in the love of God, we can face and conquer all the areas of life. Fear of facing these things in our own life has been a great contributor to our need to control. As long as we controlled others, we appeared to be right.

While all this may seem overwhelming, the fact is, this is the doorway to real relationships. In every relationship, we all have to change and grow. If we only stay in the relationships that are comfortable, we will never be challenged, and we will never grow.

Along with our release from control, we must release others from our expectation. There is probably nothing that creates more rejection than imposed expectations. Our expectations say to others that they are unacceptable the way they are. Not only can there be no relationship when expectations are imposed, there can be no appreciation or recognition of current strengths and abilities.

All of this will simply leave us in a vacuum if we don't replace it with something. Indeed, all of these codependent tendencies arise out of a lack of depending on and trusting God. In Philippians, Paul said *"Be careful for nothing; but in every thing by prayer and supplication with thanksgiving let your requests be made known unto God."* Philippians 4:6.

He didn't tell you to ignore your problems, he said not to become anxious about them. When we face any difficulties, we must manage the emotions that arise. We can try to ignore them. We can think about the problems. We can do many destructive codependent things. Or, we can present them to God.

Paul said we should present them with thanksgiving. This is not a formula about how to trick God into answering our prayer. We can present our concerns with thanksgiving because we are confident that we already have everything that pertains to life and godliness. We are thankful, because we already have what we need. What we need is not the power of God in our circumstances, we need the power of God working in our heart. We have the power of God in us right now.

Freedom from codependency comes not when we quit doing all the wrong things. Freedom from codependency doesn't even come from simply doing the right things. Freedom from codependency comes when we trust God.

We must trust God with the people around us. We must allow Him to do in their life what He wants, not what we want. We must trust God for our own personal joy and peace. We must make Him our source of security and stability. Then, and only then, are we truly free from codependency.

---

[1] *My Church My Family: How To Have a Healthy Relationship With A Church*, Dr. James B. Richards, Impact Ministries, Huntsville, Alabama

29

BREAKING THE CYCLE

Even after an individual gets the courage and the grace to break out of his individual codependent patterns, there is another major hurdle. Our codependency always involves others. Every person in our life is a player in the problem. Everyone around us has found their "nitch."

We only know how to relate to one another in our codependent, manipulative ways. We don't know any other way. Therefore, when we change, we throw everyone's life into chaos. Or, we actually come out of chaos into order. The problem is, we understand the chaos, but we don't understand the order. If it's not dysfunctional, we don't know how to live with it. All we have ever known is what we have had.

When we change, everyone around us is placed in unfamiliar territory. They've never tried to live in this arena. They have prayed for this to happen. They may have despised us the way we were. But when this change comes, they may resist it "tooth and nail." Just because we are ready, does not mean they are ready.

I remember a woman who desperately wanted her husband to get saved. He was verbally and emotionally abusive and had made her life miserable. For years, she had prayed for him and trusted God that he would get saved and change.

When he finally gave his life to the Lord, it brought about their divorce. When she got what she had been praying for, she "blew out." As illogical as that sounds, I have seen it happen many times. She had become comfortable with her dysfunctional lifestyle. She had found her way to use it to her advantage. She used guilt and nagging as a way to control her husband. She used sympathy as a way to control her friends.

When he got saved and changed dramatically, it meant she had to get a life of her own. She could no longer use his dysfunction as her identity. It meant that her unacceptable, unscriptural way of using the situation was now exposed. She could not hide her sins in the shadow of his more extreme sins. So, she divorced him. The years of verbal and emotional abuse stopped. The one thing she never expected happened. He got saved and changed. But this exposed her dysfunction.

A dominating parent can attempt to break out of the control cycle that has been imposed upon the children. Although the children have criticized and complained for years, they will not allow that parent to break free of the cycle. After all, if the parent breaks free, who will the children have to blame for their problems? The dysfunctional life style, as painful as it is, is a cycle that the children know how to work.

A dysfunctional family usually has a "strong" member. The strong member is the one that the family turns to in times of crisis. This part is not the dysfunction. After the crisis, the dysfunction arises. When the strong one of a family helps solve the problem, he/she is then accused of being a trouble maker, trying to control. The help or advise that was given, is viewed as control once the crisis is over.

Sometimes, the strong one is a full blown codependent that has a savior mentality, a "fix it complex." Sometimes, the strong one really loves and cares for the family, but doesn't know the value in establishing boundaries and breaking destructive patterns.

Whatever the case, when the strong one attempts to break the pattern, the real dysfunction will be revealed. All of the family may criticize the strong one, yet they have no intention of letting that person out of the cycle. Who would they go to for help? Other people would not be drawn into their game. Who would they blame for their problems? If they have no one to blame, they may have to deal with some responsibility. How would they manipulate the strong one? They don't believe that people really do things out of love.

I have often seen more conflict in a family when a member attempts to break free from the cycle of codependency. If a dysfunctional family member breaks free from the cycle, the rest of the family will no longer know how to control that person. Remember, control is the basic need of the codependent. They will give up the relationship before they will give up control.

When we come out of the destructive codependent style, we must be sensitive to the needs that exist around us. But we must refuse to love on their terms. We must refuse to cross the boundaries of others. We must also establish some of our own boundaries that we will not allow others to cross.

Because the codependent is so sensitive to guilt, it could be easy for others to manipulate us into showing our love in an unscriptural way. Guilt is the weapon of choice for the controller. They save it for last. Sometimes it is preceded by anger, rejection, and even violence. When all that fails, it is straight to guilt. They try to use guilt to draw us back into the codependent relationship.

We must refuse to do for others what should happen between them and God. We should be careful not to take that position in an unloving way. It is important to reaffirm love and worth, but we must only yield to Biblical concepts of love.

The frightening thing about breaking the cycle, is that we can't predict the outcome for those around us. We really don't know how they will react. We have no Biblical promise that if we do the right thing, everyone else will. Walking in true love is not an acceptable form of manipulation. It doesn't come with a guarantee of results. If it did, it would just be another form of control.

This is the most challenging part. By our breaking out of the cycle, we are creating the only real opportunity for relationship with those around us. But they may not want it. They may view our breaking free as the ultimate betrayal. "We were happy the way things were. Why did you mess it up?" What they don't know is they were the only ones who were happy. They don't see how bad it really was. They are not where you are and you cannot expect them to be.

Faith is not necessarily believing God for a specific outcome. You can't work faith for someone else. Faith is your response of trust to God and His promises to you. It is not what you can believe God to do in someone else's heart. You want the relationships around you to be saved. You want to see true love and wholeness abound with those who have been in your life. But, it may never happen.

While you can't believe God for everyone else, you can believe God's Word for you. Your trust of God is not for a specific outcome, but for a specific victory.

Regardless of what everyone else does, you know you can have personal victory. God is the source for your happiness. He is the source of your security. Other people cannot determine your future joy. Only you and God can determine this.

Personal dreams should be that, personal. We have looked to our future and we have placed the people we love into our dreams. We have determined the role they will play in our future happiness. While all of this sounds good and brings a lump to the throat of any person who longs for a life of true love, it is a part of the codependent fantasy.

There is a way that we link people to our future happiness that can be very destructive. It is often a part of our need to control them. It is often a part of why we stay in an abusive, destructive relationship. We have linked our future happiness to someone in our life.

I look forward to growing old with my wife. It is difficult to imagine life without her. It would be an unbelievably painful experience to lose her through death or relational conflict. I do envision us playing with our grandchildren. I see us spending our life together, but I also have personal dreams.

My personal dreams are about me, my life, my ministry, and the things I intend to accomplish with my life. While I see her in that picture, this has to do with me and God. I will fulfill my commitments to the Lord regardless of who is there and who isn't.

There is an unhealthy way that we link people to our personal goals that make us feel that if we lose that person, we cannot fulfill those goals. We never made them the source in a deliberate way, but because we brought them into our personal goals, we linked them in such a way that it seems impossible to fulfill those goals without them.

Every person should have their own personal dreams and goals. We should recognize how others can share those dreams with us, but not be dependent on them. After all, we need to let them have their own dreams.

Coming out of codependency is not the changing of one belief or action; it is the changing of a life-philosophy. Our entire life's motives are changed by the changing of our source. Because codependency involves everyone around us, our freedom will also involve everyone around us.

30

LIFE ON NEW TERMS

For the first time in our lives, we get to find out what it really means to live the adventure of life. We have the opportunity to experience God to the fullest. Obstacles become challenges. Threats become adventures. With God as our source, we can meet life on different terms.

There is no specified destination where we say, "I have arrived." Victory is not a destination, it is a process. In fact, life itself is a process. There is no mystical plane that we reach whereby we never have problems. We daily go through the process of trusting God and for the first time we have the opportunity to enjoy the ride.

How wonderful to know that God accepts me where I am. I know I have changes that need to come and there are still areas of my life where I want growth, but I am comfortable with me. Since I don't have a destination, I am comfortable on the ride. Since I don't have a destination, I can be happy with where I am today.

With one eye, I look to the future, expectant of positive changes in my life and character. On the other hand, I am satisfied with where I am today. It is not my responsibility to change. It is merely my responsibility to be open to change as the Holy Spirit brings it into my life.

Life is continual change. When we stop

changing, we die. Even if we found the perfect relationship, it would require change to maintain it. Every relationship changes as people and circumstances change. Therefore, we must change to stay in step with the relationship.

So, change is no longer motivated from the feeling of lack, deficiency, or need. Change is no longer negative or threatening. Change is the way I stay in the flow of life. Change is the process whereby I stay capable of enjoying life to its fullest. Change is really my friend. I don't change because I am wrong, I change because I am alive and I exist in a dynamic, changing environment.

Life in Jesus is easy and light. Freedom from the need to become, yet open to change. It doesn't get any easier than this. I am, therefore, I change into who I am. I do not become by changing. I change because I am. I am righteous, in Him. I am anointed, in Him. I am in Jesus.

I determine to be satisfied and comfortable with who I am in Jesus. I can't be who you want me to be. I can't live for your expectations. I can only be who I am, in Jesus. If that is not good enough for those around me, they must take that up with my Father. This is not an excuse to be rude, inconsiderate, or unloving. It is the reality that we all must live with. I am who I am today and that's all I can be.

I am going to let you be who you are. If you want to be who you are in Jesus, that's fine. If that's not what you want, that's your choice. No matter how much I disagree with that choice, it is still your choice, not mine. Who we choose to yield our lives to, may mean we drift apart, or it may mean we draw closer. I will love you wherever it takes us, but I will not assume the need to make this friendship come out a certain way.

I must let Jesus be your Lord, just as you must allow Him to be mine. He is the One you must follow. If you follow Him and I follow Him, we will ultimately arrive at the proper destination. You are His servant, not mine. One thing for sure, if we are following Him, we will walk in love throughout our journey.

If I make you into the person I want you to be, you will never have your own life and you'll never find your own destiny. If you're the person I want you to be, you can't be the person you want to be. If your life is revolving around me and my desires, it can never revolve around Jesus. Thus, my control ensures you will never be happy, because you will look to me to make you happy. However, if I set you free to find your happiness in Jesus, you will look to Him as your source.

With God at the center of your life, for the first time, your life will be secure. All that you do will flow out of the confidence that comes from being a child of God. He will be your source. He will be your confidence. Religion will have no place in you. You will only have room for the pure, undefiled love of God that you can feel; the love that makes you feel good about yourself and your God.

With a heart full of the love of God, you will be free from the manipulation of man. Others can affect you, but they can't control you. They can wound you, but they can't destroy you. They can bend you, but they cannot break you. Trying to hurt you would be like stealing a cup of water from the ocean. It's no big loss.

Once you have tasted the goodness of God for yourself, you are hooked for life. You've got the ultimate addiction, the real deal, the genuine craving, but you're satisfied. As the Psalmist said, *"Oh that men would praise the LORD for his goodness, and for his wonderful works to the children of men! For he satisfieth the longing soul, and filleth the hungry soul with goodness."* Psalms 107:8-9.

The rest of your life will be a journey of experiencing the goodness of God. Enjoy the trip!